Lost Loot

Lost Loot

Ghostly New England Treasure Tales

by Patricia Hughes

Schiffer Publishing Ltd®

4880 Lower Valley Road, Atglen, Pennsylvania 19310

Dedication

This book is dedicated to my family and friends, who have supported my writing throughout the years. Their support and encouragement is appreciated more than words can say. It is true that without them, this book may have forever remained unwritten.

Published by Schiffer Publishing Ltd.
4880 Lower Valley Road
Atglen, PA 19310
Phone: (610) 593-1777; Fax: (610) 593-2002
E-mail: Info@schifferbooks.com

For the largest selection of fine reference books on this and related subjects, please visit our web site at
www.schifferbooks.com. We are always looking for people to write books on new and related subjects. If you have an idea for a book please contact us at the above address.

This book may be purchased from the publisher.
Include $3.95 for shipping.
Please try your bookstore first.
You may write for a free catalog.

In Europe, Schiffer books are distributed by
Bushwood Books
6 Marksbury Ave.
Kew Gardens
Surrey TW9 4JF England
Phone: 44 (0) 20 8392-8585; Fax: 44 (0) 20 8392-9876
E-mail: info@bushwoodbooks.co.uk
Website: www.bushwoodbooks.co.uk
Free postage in the U.K., Europe; air mail at cost.

Designed by Mark David Bowyer
Type set in Burton's Nightmare 2000 / NewBaskerville BT

ISBN: 978-0-7643-2816-9
Printed in China

Contents

Introduction

Location, Location, Location!

Those words really mean everything when one begins to search for lost treasure. The question to really ask is why does it seem that there are only certain places that have multiple treasure sites with a supernatural occurrence, while other areas have no lost treasure stories at all? Is it just a coincidence, or perhaps merely a convenience for the person burying the treasure, or is it a convincing argument that certain places have an aura that invite secrets? Was it the era that convinced people to bury their loot in these selected locations? Northern New England was the fringe, a vast and unknown frontier at one time. Pirates and smugglers are only a few of the parties that buried loot in this region. What better place to bury savings, or hide ill gotten gains, or to find valuable minerals and gems, than in an area with raging rivers, huge waterfalls, high mountains, and vast infinite forests that had no real trail through them, or small islands to find shelter from pursuing ships? Who would ever think to look for lost treasures in those places?

Whatever the true reason, the fact remains that Maine, New Hampshire, and Vermont have numerous treasures that have been hidden and are guarded by strange and mysterious spirits, or haunted by death or curses to those who may have found them. Some of the treasures caches have been discovered, but many still remain in the earth today. To further safeguard the buried loot, one could just throw a curse on it, or have a phantom guardian always maintain a vigil over the site. It is really no wonder that certain places become enchanted and magical, complete with a treasure adventure and a roaming ghost that awaits the daring seeker.

Within these pages, the mystical tales will become the adventure to explore northern New England's treasure and ghost stories for those who dare. The lost loot and supernatural tales are intertwined, one thread winding slowly into the next, and one truly can not be told without the other. The stories are an unique voyage through New England's enchanted, supernatural, and treasure-laden history. The ending is still not complete, and will remain a mystery, until all the treasures still lost have been found.

Chapter One
Where is the Golden City in Northern New England?

Riches May be in the Eye of the Beholder

Ghost and treasure stories are intertwined in the lore of New England. Buildings erected with pure gold, shining brightly in the burning mid-day sun, gem-encrusted people and jewelry form the ancient legends. Stone-sized gems and nuggets are found lying on the ground for the taking; these fabulous stories are what caused many Europeans to brave the unknown Atlantic Ocean, and cross to the new world to settle a new land in the sixteenth century.

Sometimes the stories and places were actually true, and there *were* gold-covered buildings and stone-sized gems to be found. Though more often than not, the stories were just tall tales and yarns spun by seamen who wanted to share their great adventures of a new world with a spellbound audience, or a way for the Native American people to get the Europeans settlers to move quickly to another place. The barrier between myth and truth is hard to break, and to add to the mystery and magic, the many buried treasure stories in this region are filled with ghostly or supernatural encounters.

It may be hard to believe, but treasure was being sought in New England before the Europeans officially discovered the area. There was no doubt that the new world held riches beyond any European's dreams, and the gold and silver that was pouring out of South America into the treasury of Spain could not be denied. It was assumed by most people of the time, that if there were riches in South America, then it was possible, and even probable, that the same riches were to be found in North America. That was not necessarily the truth.

The quest for New England treasure is said to have been started in the early sixteenth century with an English seaman named David Ingram. He was stranded in the Gulf of Mexico, after the Spanish fleet attacked and destroyed his ship. It is also true that he was known for telling the great yarn, and he had no great love of the Spanish who captured him.

The Spanish were well-known at the time for taking unbelievable amounts of riches from South America and Mexico. Probably to save his life, Seaman Ingram told his captors of a fantastic city, located two thousand miles, give or take a few hundred miles, to the north. He told of the lost city of Norumbega in the wilderness of northern New England. (By the way, this area was not called New England at that time, it was not even really known to England or Europe.) He described in detail the community where houses had crystal entrances and each home had a roof made of gold and silver. The streets, he said, were studded with pearls and a gold-lined river ran through the city, where nuggets could be picked up while walking along the shore. The residents of this fabled land, wore fur garments, and had large jewels adorning them, which included rubies that were four inches long and two inches broad. It was an amazing place, and Ingram held the Spanish in awe and longing with his tale.

Supposedly, Ingram had traveled down to the Gulf of Mexico from this area, so he was describing something that he saw personally. Perhaps he was telling the Spanish exactly what they wanted to hear, and who could blame him? He did manage to escape, and made it back to England. However, in England, where he was not a captured victim, he told the same story. Perhaps he was a great storyteller, who loved to exaggerate, or perhaps he was just lying, hoping his listeners would spend time, money, and energy searching for the non-existent city. Whatever his reasons were, Norumbega or Norumbegue is first used as a real place on the map by the Spanish and Portuguese early voyages to the New England coast. This tale may never have existed if the Native American word was known and translated correctly. In the Algonkin language, Norumbega meant "a quiet place between two rapids."

Jean Alfonse, the pilot of the ship, *Roberval*, mentions the name in his logs, and he is also the first person to navigate the waters of Massachusetts Bay. Norumbega is supposedly thirty degrees from the coast, up a river, where the coast turns to the west and northwest for more than two hundred and fifty leagues.

Jean Parmentier, a Frenchman, also brought the story back to Europe in the early 1500s. He described that he actually saw "the golden, gem encrusted city that laid only fifteen leagues from the coast up the river." Whatever he actually saw, or exaggeration he may have told, it is noted by others at the time that he was also a great storyteller.

After the story circulated in Europe, Simon Ferdinardo, a Portuguese seaman, decided it was time to go on the quest to find this golden place, but to his utter amazement, he failed to find the fabled city. No one could understand what had happened. It was thought that perhaps Ferdinardo just searched in the wrong place.

In 1604, Samuel de Champlain, finally put an end to the golden city search. He did not find any golden city on his historic voyage up the Penobscot River in Maine, but he did find good people living there, and they had plenty of different types of furs to sell to a willing European market. Champlain liked the Native Americans that he met here, and they called this river the Kenduskeag. Champlain came to believe that Norumbega was not an actual city, but the river itself. The river was large, spacious, and had many islands. This is why he put the name Norumbega for the Penobscot River on his map in 1612.

The French erected a fort, in 1656, on the ancient spot where Norumbega supposedly stood. They called it Fort Norumbega, as a tribute to the ancient golden city that was said to be seen with shining towers and domes by those early travelers. It is interesting to ask what *was* that shining object that could have been seen by early explorers? Was it a mass hallucination or a great mirage, or were they seeing exactly what they wanted to see, or, as will be explored in future chapters, is there something still unknown that shines from a distance in New England?

Norumbega is the earliest name for the city of Bangor, Maine. That is supposedly where the fabled city was located on early maps. In fact, if one looked at the actual directions given for this mythical city, and if any accounts of this fabled city were true, then the actual location was on the east side of the river, not the west side of the river. That would make Brewer, Maine, the golden city— not Bangor.

Maine's Lost Native Americans

Just to make this story even more interesting, there is a lost Native American tribe story that is connected to the lost city of Norumbega. The tribe is called the Wawenoc and was once considered one of the six primary tribes in early Maine history. They are not in any modern history book about early Maine, so the question becomes *why?* The most well-known native of this tribe is called Samoset, the same Native American who greeted the Pilgrims when they landed in Massachusetts. He also greeted the Europeans by speaking English. It is said that he was a member of the Wawenoc tribe from Muscongus Island.

The Wawenoc tribe were Abenaki, whose principle villages were the estuaries down river from the modern-day towns of Liberty and Montville in Waldo County. This could have been what the Native Americans considered part of the Norumbega backcountry, which was a major hunting area of the Abenaki. The lost village was called Muskingum or "The Kingdom," which is the Algonquin word meaning, "elk's eyes, deer eyes." The backcountry roads that still exist today, basically follow those prehistoric hunting trails.

The question to understanding what may have happened to the Wawenoc tribe lies in considering what the word Norumbega really means. The name in Algonquin means, "a quiet place between two rapids." In the Abenaki language, the name means, "a stretch of quiet water between two rapids or a succession of rapids interspersed by still waters.". According to history, at least European history, the name was the golden northern city that rivaled the South American cities where gold was found. Perhaps the name is really the difference between two cultures.

Norumbega was a very real place, a place where great fortune of game for food could be found in the vast hunting grounds to the Natives living here. That may have translated, or have been communicated badly, to finding a fortune in the golden mythical city to the Europeans.

Norumbega was the bioregion of the Wawenoc tribe. This was a large area that started from Cape Elizabeth northward and eastward to just beyond Mount Desert Island. It is said that the famous chief, or Sagamore, Bashabas, lived here. It is clear that this region between the Kennebec and Penobscot

Rivers must have had significant impact on the life of the Native Americans living in Maine. It must have had a name. Is it just a coincidence that the domain of the Wawenoc people, almost exactly matches the cartography of the region of Norumbega on European maps?

There are references of the tribe found until 1617. The answer to the question of what happened and why they were no longer considered an ancient tribe in modern Maine history might be twofold. One reason may be that there was a major and deadly war between the Micmacs and Wawenocs in 1607. There were many deaths in the Wawenoc tribe, and this decrease in population allowed the Etchemin tribe to move into the niche left by the dying Wawenoc tribe.

The second reason may be that a great epidemic spread through the remainder of the tribe, obliterating them from history between 1609 and 1617. By the time the Europeans began to keep records of this area, the tribe had simply completely disappeared. Any survivors may have become part of another tribe in the area. It is thought that the survivors settled in Beacancout and St. Francois, and perhaps became part of the St. Francis tribe in Canada. In 1914, the last known Wawenoc tribe member was interviewed in Becancour, Quebec, by Frank Speck.

It would appear that this would be the end of the Wawenoc story, but three hundred years ago at Merrymeeting Bay, a legend arose. The story goes that after the long battle, the Wawenoc tribe started to wander throughout the land. The chief of the tribe, Assonimo, decided that some of the Wawenoc tribe members who wanted to live in Maine, should do so. A small group of the Wawenoc settled on the Bomba-hook Stream, which at that time, emptied into the Kennebec River at Hallowell. They settled on the north bank, where there was plenty of fish to eat.

The European settlers in the region, however, were not happy to have this war-weary tribe too close to them. Assonimo asked to meet with the settlers. The Europeans attended the meeting, and the peace pipe was passed between them. All smoked, talked, and the night passed slowly.

Assonimo told the settlers that his tribe was tired of war and death. They just wanted to settle down in the land they loved. They wanted to have a safe place to hunt, fish, and have children. The tribe offered to hunt and fish for the settlers, if they would just let them live here.

Life was not easy in the frontier of Maine, and the settlers liked this idea. They offered to pay for the food with blankets and ammunition. The Wawenoc liked this idea and a peaceful coexistence was established.

Peace reigned for a long time. It was a hot, humid, hazy summer day when a bad storm came down from the hills. The settlers would call these storms, wind falls or cyclones. The storm swept straight through the Native American settle-ment. After the storm passed, the settlers quickly went to the camp to help, but no one was there. The settlers never found a single body.

The settlers mourned for their lost friends. As time passed, pine trees grew over the old Wawenoc village. One day, one of the settlers who knew the Wawenoc story, counted the trees and remarked that this was the exact number of people in the tribe. He even claimed that one of the trees was smoking, and that it reminded him of the peace pipe that they had shared years before.

The Smoking Pines were witnessed by people living in the area as late as 1888. The Pines seemed to give off a vapor from the top, and no one could explain why. The people in the area believed it was a sign that the Wawenocs finally found roots in the land that they loved.

Follow That Dream!

The question always seems to arise of exactly who discovered New England. That question will be explored in future chapters. The more interesting question here is really why was North America discovered? Was it for the thrill of exploration, a grand adventure to talk about with friends and family, or was it just to settle somewhere new to start a new life? The truth may be none of the above. The very real answer is because of simple economics.

The truth is found in an old expression; "Gold follows the sun." Europeans followed that dream and they headed west from their homes, the way the sun sets, and they hoped to discover a new land, filled with riches beyond what they could have ever hoped to find. What they found was a vast unknown, with high mountains, raging rivers, and desolate islands. What existed in that vast, dark, and scary region was terrifying to the first explorers. If great treasure did exist, it would not be easy to find or keep. No wonder so many enchanted and deadly legends sprung to life in this region. Many people did die while trying to find this lost loot, so the treasure may actually be somewhat tainted and haunted.

What one does notice is that treasure and ghost stories seem to be located in certain areas. There seems to be more than one story in any given locale. Why this is true is unknown, but it does lend credence to why certain places are blessed with hidden treasure, but also haunted with ghosts and monsters protecting the loot. Not all areas have treasure and ghost tales, but where there are tales, they are usually numerous.

Within these pages are the dark and brilliant stories of these treasure hunts, some were successful, some are documented fact, and some are oral legends told since the beginning of time. Many treasures were found with a price, and those are the dark tales told by the campfire in the dead of a New England night. They are, and will be always, connected, and one story can not be told without the other. So, here begins the first treasure hunt in New England, but it certainly was not the last. Though some hunts may have ended with no loot actually being found, there have been other hunts where the lost treasure has been discovered.

Three Tales

Ocean Born Mary of Henniker

There are three ghostly treasure tales of northern New England that do not have a particular island or mountain associated with them. They are unique to the region, so since there is a treasure to be found, and a ghost to beware, it seemed only fitting that they were added to this book.

This pirate love story is well-known as the Ocean Born Mary of Henniker, New Hampshire tale. The story begins in Londonberry, Ireland in 1720. Life was hard in Ireland, so Mary's parents decided to come to America to start a new life. As the ship neared Boston Harbor, Elizabeth Wilson, Mary's mother, went into labor and gave birth. While she was in labor, the ship was attacked by pirates. The pirate leader was called Don Pedro. After boarding the ship, he ordered all the passengers to be killed, while he looked for the rich cargo on board.

Just before his order could be carried out, he heard the baby cry. The story goes that once he saw Mary, he made a very strange request. If the parents named their baby after his mother, Mary, he would spare the passengers. He also gave the parents a green dress that Mary would have to wear on her wedding day. Obviously, Mary's parents quickly agreed, and the pirates left with all the loot, but not killing anyone.

Here's where the story starts to unwind. Mary grew up and was happily married to James Wallace. She is said to have had a great life, and had five children, but became a widow shortly after the birth of her fifth child. Don Pedro is said to have retired from being a pirate, and built a home in New Hampshire. (By the way, he is the only pirate ever recorded to have successfully retired from piracy).

The ending of a pirate's career is usually much more violent, as will be discussed in future chapters. However, it is said that he looked for Mary, found her a widow, married her, and brought her to New Hampshire to live. Life is said to have been good, her children grew up, and settled near their mother.

One day, she saw Don Pedro with other men, carrying a large black trunk into the orchard in back of the house. He told Mary that when he died, he wanted to be buried with the treasure that was buried under the hearthstone in their home. Don Pedro was later stabbed in the orchard, and it is said that Mary buried her husband with his treasure under the hearthstone in her home. When Mary died in 1814, it is said that she started to haunt the house, perhaps to keep others from finding the treasure, or perhaps just wanting to be near Don Pedro.

The problem is that, apparently, Mary never lived in the house that she is said to haunt. It belonged to her son, Robert. Mary also never lived in Henniker until she was seventy-eight years old. She moved there to live with another son, William.

However, never fear; all is not lost with this story—it does have an interesting twist. Apparently, Don Pedro really did grow tired of the pirate life. Since it is not easy to retire as a pirate, during one of his last raids on a ship, it is said that he spared the Wallace's lives, if they would say he was their son, James. So, if this is true, Mary did actually marry her pirate, and this pirate did have loot, so who knows where the pirate may have buried his treasure.

General Jonathan Moulton

The second tale takes place in Hampton, New Hampshire. It is really more of a folk tale, but it is a supernatural treasure folk tale. General Jonathan Moulton was known as a great warrior throughout New England in an earlier time.

The only vice he was said to have was that he liked money a bit too much. One day, he made the comment that he would not mind selling his soul to the devil, if only he could be filthy rich and never have to worry about money again.

The devil, it is said, decided to take him up on his offer. It was agreed that the devil would fill the General's boots with gold the first day of each month, if he would give the devil his soul when he died. The General went out and bought the largest boots he could find. As agreed, the devil filled those boots with gold.

Now, the General believed that he could outsmart the devil. He cut the bottom of the boots out, and every time the Devil tried to fill the boots, they would not reach the top. The gold just kept falling out of the bottom of the boots. Soon, the entire room was filled with gold. It is said that the Devil was not happy with the General.

Later that night, the story continues, the General's house mysteriously burned down, with his boots still in them, and the deal was now null and void. It is said that the General searched the area for the large lump of gold that must be there. Gold can be melted, but fire cannot destroy it! The General was left with nothing. He died with no money, wondering what happened to his large lump of solid gold. It must be somewhere in the vicinity of his burned home.

When he died, there were so many rumors about his contract with the devil, that the authorities opened his grave to quiet the rumors, but to their surprise the grave was empty. Where the gold and the General are to this day remains a mystery.

The *Dash*

The third ghostly treasure tale is about a cursed ship that roams Maine's coastline. In 1812, the privateer, *Dash*, was the fastest ship in the province of Maine, perhaps on the entire American coast. The *Dash* was built at Porter's Landing in Freeport by master shipbuilder, James Brewer, who was commissioned by the shipyard owned by the Porter Brothers.

The War of 1812 had taken its toll on shipbuilding in the Freeport area. Shipping was completely disrupted because of the war. There was no foreign trade, and any ships that tried to trade along the coast were usually plundered. As a result, no new sloops or schooners were being ordered or built. Business was very bad and there were no real prospects for it getting better in the near future.

At first, the Porters had Brewer outfit the *Dash* as a schooner, with sixteen guns, and sent her out of the harbor. On her maiden voyage, the ship sprung a foremast, and then it was converted to a brig. What that meant was that it was now a two-master, squared-rigged forward and a schooner-rigged aft. It may have been a hybrid ship, but the *Dash* could, and did, outrun any British ship that chased it.

In the two years that the *Dash* cruised the coast from Portland, Maine to Bermuda, to Port-au-Prince and North Carolina, the crew captured fifteen ships. The *Dash* was the first ship to be commissioned by the United States in the War of 1812. In November 1814, Captain John Porter and his crew of sixty men sailed out of Portland Harbor and captured three schooners, one sloop, and three brigs. The *Dash* was considered a great ship.

In January 1815, the *Dash* once again sailed out of Portland Harbor in the company of another ship, the *Champlain*, and sailed into history. The Captain of the *Champlain* said they lost sight of the *Dash* six hours out on the first night. No trace was ever found of the *Dash*, nor has any of her crew been seen since. Or perhaps that is not the total story and the ship *has* been seen again.

The official story is that a bad storm came up that night and drove the *Dash* onto George's Bank, where the strong tide sent the ship to a watery grave very quickly. However, legend and residents along the coastline have claimed to see the *Dash* in the waters long after it went down. This is not a happy sighting. It seems that one may only see the *Dash* when death is close by. Only those with an ancestor who was lost on the *Dash* can see it as it winds through the water, but never coming to port. The sighting signals that death is lurking and to be cautious.

As an interesting side note, as famous as the *Dash* was and as much treasure as the crew brought home from its raids, there are no actual known drawings or paintings of the *Dash*—yet the sightings all describe the same things about the seen ship.

The coast of New England has hundreds of islands because it is a drowned coastline. This phenomena was caused by the heavy weight of the glaciers. The tops of hills and mountains never completely rebounded when the glaciers receded, so the numerous islands were created. Because of the various islands here, pirates frequented these places, mainly to hide from the authorities, and to hide their ill-gotten gains from others. It is easier to run around an island and hide in a cove, than to run away from pursuers in the open sea.

X Marks the Spot

The first pirate documented in New England was Dixie or Dixey Bull, and he started his career as a pirate in Machias Bay, just off the coast of Maine. Treasure is said to still be hidden in these remote places, and the first part of this book will discuss and describe what islands may still harbor pirate treasure. Before picking up a shovel and heading toward the coast however, it would be a good idea to note that these stories also contain the curses and ghosts that still remain protecting the lost loot.

There are four islands in Maine called Treasure Island—for the obvious reason. There is a legend in each case that states that there is buried treasure on the islands. One is in Cumberland County, near Gray, on Little Sebago Lake. The second is in Piscataquis County on Moosehead Lake. The third is in Washington County on Grand Lake and the last is in Hancock County, near Sorrento. The island near Sorrento is also called, Doanes Island, Soward Island, or Sewards Island. The details are vague about who or what type of treasure is buried on the island, but it also could be that no one ever really knew what type of treasure was here to try to keep the amount a secret.

There are five Gold Brooks in Maine, and gold was found in all five of those waterways. The first one runs in Hancock County, near Orland. The second is in Oxford County, near Bowman. The third is in Franklin County, near the Kibby Stream near Dallas. The fourth is in Somerset County, near the Chase Stream Tract. The last is in Knox County, near Appleton. There is also an island called Spirit Island on Lower Richardson Lake in Oxford County that is said to be haunted—or perhaps guarding something that is precious buried on the island?

The second part of this book will discuss the three main mountain regions of northern New England and the treasure and spirits that may still be hidden under the rock. The three mountain regions are the Longfellow or Blue Mountains in western Maine, the White Mountains of New Hampshire, and the Green Mountain of Vermont. These areas are rich in treasure history and spirit lore. The Native Americans were excellent miners and some of their mines have never been found. There are treasures buried by the military, Spanish, Native Americans, settlers, smugglers, and bandits in all three locations, and many of the locations are guarded by ghosts or supernatural beings. We will explore the highest elevations of the region and discover why there are so many unique gems that are only found in this area, deep in the folded mountains of the Appalachian Range.

Now, onto the quest for supernatural buried treasure…

Chapter Two
Pirates and the New England Coast

Whenever one is seeking treasure, the very first thing that comes to mind is pirates' buried treasure. The tropical island with the white sandy beach, complete with a full glowing moon overhead and the ocean quietly lapping on the shore in the distance is the perfect place for *X* to mark the treasure spot. The muffled curses and sound of shovels digging in the sand, as well as the grunting of the eye-patched men with golden earrings and parrots on their shoulders, is heard, as a heavy chest is lowered below the sand. The scream of the crew member chosen to guard the treasure echoes through the night, as he falls into the treasure pit, dying from his Captain's knife or gun wound. After some time passes, the quiet sounds of paddling are heard, then the sound grows softer and softer until it finally disappears forever. That is the typical scene of a pirate and his buried treasure—or so many believe.

The colder New England islands and coast have seen their share of pirates though. The very first pirate to roam in North America got his start in Machias Bay, Maine. He was called Dixie Bull, sometimes spelled *Dixey Bull*. To understand where a pirate may bury a treasure, it would help to know what a New England pirate was, and why he or she, may have actually wanted to bury treasure along the New England coast, thereby leaving it behind for another to hopefully find.

Pirates have roamed the seas since ancient Greece and are found all over the world, even today. In New England, many so-called pirates were really privateers. There was no navy in the early days of New England. There was no protective agency that roamed the seas during those times. It was also well known that Spain was taking much gold and silver out of South America and that their ships were loaded with treasure. It was a long way back to Spain and the Atlantic Ocean was huge and dangerous.

Other European nations wanted a part of this treasure, but no one nation wanted to officially go against the mighty Spanish fleet. So, protection was given by proxy, and the United States government would have to hire help. That is the difference between a pirate and a privateer. A pirate is one who plunders and robs any ship on the sea. A privateer is an armed vessel that is licensed to seize and attack vessels of a hostile nation. The privateer carried documents or licenses, called a "Letter of Marque and Reprisal." This gave the privateer permission to pirate other ships from the hostile government. They would have to give part of their "take" to the government who gave them permission to take plunder from another ship. In return, they would get some of the loot stolen, titles, land, and perhaps even a ship of their own. Many pirates in New England started as privateers, but became wanted pirate crews eventually.

Pirates roamed the New England coast for almost fifty years unchecked. The heyday for pirates was in the year 1720, but the pirate era did not end until the nineteenth century, when the United States Navy finally ended their reign. The first United States Navy was actually made up of colonial cruisers searching for pirates and protecting merchant ships from them.

The word *pirate* comes from the Greek word, *peiran*, which means to attack. In the seventeenth and eighteenth centuries, the pirate was known by many names, "the outlaw of the sea," "a marine freebooter," or "a marine knight." When a seaman became a pirate, it was said that he or she went out to sea or was going on the account. Whatever they were called, they all worked on the same principle: "no prey, no pay." Any ship under any flag was fair game to a pirate.

A pirates' life was fleeting and held very cheap. The crew members' average age was twenty-seven years old. The feeling was that life was cheap not only included the crewman's life, but the lives of their victims. It was not a glamorous life, but the promise of adventure, gold, and all the good things in life, was better then any other type of life at sea at that time. Life was hard, and the chance to make money, was usually worth the price. The life expectancy of a pirate was very short. All pirates that were captured and convicted were hanged. Though it was dangerous to get caught, it was actually very rare. In the early days, pirates were considered a privileged criminal class. There is no argument that many pirates were not very good people, but even during their own lifetime, they were admired as romantic heroes. It is not hard to see where the Hollywood movie pirate came from.

It may be hard to believe, but pirate ships did have laws that the crew would follow. Pirate crews operated under a document that was considered a constitution. Before each voyage, each crew drew up and signed the articles, based on earlier regulations from the pirates or buccaneers. These articles were sworn to on the Bible, usually with a lot of rum to go around after everyone signed. No two pirate articles were the same. Examples of articles may include: that a crew member could enter the captains' cabin anytime he wanted, or that they could even swear at him. Another example would be that they could take what they wanted from another ship. The only real plus to being a pirate captain was that he got the largest share of the loot taken from another ship.

The captain of a pirate ship was usually tough, ruthless, and very capable of murder and torture. They were bold and decisive in action, as well as excellent navigators. They also usually swore and drank heavily. The captain was duly elected by the crew and considered a public servant to them. The only other person who was elected by the crew was the quartermaster. He was equal to the captain and actually supervised the running of the ship, except during battle. The quartermaster led the boarding parties, was in charge of the ship's stolen loot until it was divided, and was the one who meted out any punishment to the crew. The quartermaster was the only person on the ship, contrary to popular belief, that could flog a person, and then only with the support of the majority of the crew.

The captain or quartermaster could be disposed of by the vote of the crew at any time. The loot was divided equally, except that the captain received two full shares and the quartermaster received one and a half shares. Even the most famous pirates, like Blackbeard and Kidd, followed these rules.

The crew of a pirate ship usually outnumbered the crew of the victims' ship around ten to one. The crew of the other ship would hardly ever really defend the cargo that they did not own, but the pirates had to kill at least once to set an example. The reputation that the pirate ship crew may kill, was usually all that was needed to capture another ship. It made stealing the cargo easier and faster the next time.

Pirates usually did not make anyone walk the plank. Most of the time, the main punishment was to maroon the crew member. This meant that the quartermaster would put a crewmember ashore on a deserted island, usually a captured crew member, under the pretense of having committed some great crime against the pirates. This was the most effective means of punishment or revenge. The marooned victim was always left a gun, six bullets, a few pinches of gun powder, and a bottle of fresh water.

Unfortunately, the pirate torture and sadism may have been no worse than the official means of execution and torture at that time. Perhaps the pirates were just products of their era. The pirates did not write most accounts of their lives—many were illiterate—so this could be the reason for so many myths. Today, their story is only told though oral legends and official documents of trials and convictions of pirates.

A typical pirate crew shore leave was something that many coastal and island residents would like to forget. The first night on shore, the crew just got drunk. The second night, however, the crew went looking for companionship, and on the third and fourth nights, they would usually gamble away what they had stolen. Frequently, they would continue to gamble until all their loot ran out, but sometimes, they would have enough for one more night of getting drunk. It was often that they had to be carried back on board their ships for the next raid.

Believe it or not, in spite of the wild days on leave, at the turn of the seventeenth century, most British colonies welcomed the pirates. The only colonies that did not want them around were New York, Maryland, and Virginia.

Bury the Treasure, But Where?

Sometimes gold and silver bars and coins are found buried in a sack, instead of a wooden chest or kettle. The reason for this is that many of the pirates' victims, when they knew that a pirate ship was coming after them and that they would soon be boarded, would throw their valuables overboard or hide their loot in smaller sacks, making it easier to hide, rather then let the pirate get them.

Once acquiring the loot, why would a pirate bury all his ill gotten booty? There are five possible reasons:

1. When loot is found on a beach, it is usually assumed that it was buried. The truth may be that it was not, however, buried. The pirates were shipwrecked before the crew could save the loot and it was still under the ocean.

2. If the pirates were going into battle, they would bury the loot on the eve of the battle on the nearest shore.

3. If the pirates were or felt trapped, a lighter and shallower vessel might be better able to escape. They could always come back for the loot, which may have been too heavy to carry or not feasible to bring along, if they survived.

4. They had such successful cruises, that the pirates actually had to put the loot on shore for retrieval at a later date as a method of "banking" their money. There were no banks at this time, and it was the custom that many people buried their money to keep it safe. They

usually had no legitimate heirs and did not want the government to take their wealth.

5. The pirate captain would often hold out on the crew and would hide the extra loot, above his two shares, to retrieve at a later date. Captains did not want to give extra loot to the crew.

So it is a fact that pirates did bury their treasure at times, and it was usually in small caches in numerous and varied places. Legends state that when pirates bury a treasure, they always dig a hole deep enough to put in a human body that would be killed and buried with the loot. This crew member, or perhaps a slave, would be the ghostly protector for the loot—though not always willing. This is one reason that many of the ghosts that protect the treasure are not pleasant or happy to see the treasure seeker.

The pirates in this hemisphere would mainly try to capture the Spanish treasure ships. There were six to ten ships that were called the Spanish plate ships or the silver fleet. These were the ships that the treasures of the New World were sent on each year to Spain. Many of these ships were destroyed in storms and it is their coins that show up on shore every so often.

From the beginning of the sixteenth century, until well into the nineteenth century, thirty to forty million dollars worth of gold and silver were exported each year to Spain. It is not really surprising that pirates cruised the sea searching for these ships. It is also the main reason that many governments wanted their share of this treasure, too. The golden era of piracy only lasted about thirty years, from 1691 to 1724.

Pieces of Eight

It has been said that one eighth of all the treasure taken from the New World lies on the ocean floor. One half of all the refined gold of the entire world lies underwater on the ocean, lakes, and river bottoms. The pirates took an even higher percentage of the treasure that was being sent home to Spain. How much wealth was actually taken from the Americas is not really known. The treasure ships would usually undervalue their cargo because of the Royal Fifth. (This was the twenty percent tax that the Spanish Royalty put on all the treasure sent back to Spain.)

Though this may be hard to believe, pirates did not truly like fighting and would avoid it whenever possible. Taking the cargo with the least resistance as possible was always the goal. Pirates did not always try to capture ships; there are many accounts of pirates trying to salvage the wrecked Spanish treasure ships. The Spanish probably lost more in salvage, then from the pirates actually attacking their ships.

The famous violent New England storms that ravaged the coast and islands, created many a pirate salvager. The storms also killed many innocent victims. If the victim did not die as a result of the wreck, than it is probable that they were killed by the salvager, who did not want witnesses to the crimes they were committing.

The reason that pieces of eight are so connected to pirates is because the pirates attacked the Spanish treasure fleet. Pieces of eight were the common currency for trading in South and Central America and the West Indies. The coins had the Spanish Coat of Arms on one side and the Pillars of Hercules on the other. These coins were so common that the twin pillars became the two straight lines that we use today in our own dollar ($) sign. A pesos is called "eight reales" or pieces of eight. Spanish reales are silver coins and Escudos, or doubloons, are gold nuggets.

Native American craftsmen were enslaved by the Spanish to create the pieces of eight. The coins were produced in Peru, Columbia, and Mexico for over three hundred years. The craftsmen would hammer the silver to flat, irregular shapes, thus creating the coin.

Wooden Legs and Parrots

Everyone has an idea of what a pirate looks like, but in fact, there are no known pictures of a New England pirate of that era. They could, and did, have wooden legs, they actually did have parrots. The parrots were used as bribes to officials to look the other way. They did tie scarves or large handkerchiefs around their heads, and they were armed with pistols and a cutlass. The scarves were used as a disguise. They could pull it over their faces.

A pirate recognition code, as well as their flags, was shown by hoving to and firing leeward. The Jolly Roger flag, the black flag with a white skull and crossbones and the most famous pirate flag known, was not the only pirate flag. The Jolly Roger origin is obscure, but it was used as early as 1719, perhaps even earlier. The flag was a form of psychological warfare on the pirates' part.

There were also red patterned flags, to show the blood spilled by the crew. Some of the pirate flags displayed full skeletons. The skull and hourglass was a favorite of some pirates. It signified the short life span for those who saw the flag.

Edward Low had a full red skeleton flag, signifying to anyone who saw it that they would become a bloodied skeleton.

But Why?

Based on the information given in the previous pages, the question often asked is *why would anyone become a pirate?* There is just one main reason, and that again is simple economics. There was a lot of money to be taken. Unfortunately, this money came from someone else. Where they could get this money with the least amount of trouble, became the most important issue to the pirates who roamed the New England coast.

However, once the loot was stolen, a place to hide the money was also needed. How would one keep the treasure safe once buried? The answer was that the treasure needed guards who would never leave the spot for any reason. That was why many pirates are said to have killed someone to guard the Captains' treasure. Their ghosts will always guard the treasure, no matter how many years pass, and they will keep the secret to where the treasure lies when anyone comes seeking the buried loot. It is also possible that since these guards were murdered, their ghosts would not be pleasant to encounter, and that may also keep unwanted seekers from finding the treasure.

Chapter Three
Captain Kidd and New England Treasure

Over twenty different pirates have cruised the coast of New England, either hiding treasure after plundering a Spanish treasure ship or other ships, or looking for places to sell or steal more ill-gotten loot.

The next few chapters of this book will explore the lives of six of the most famous pirates that roamed New England waters; Captain Kidd, Blackbeard, Low, Quelch, Bellamy, and Dixie Bull. Of course, there are also stories about treasure buried by unknown pirates or vague stories about treasure being buried by pirates in general that exist in the region.

One example lies in the town of Prospect on the Penobscot River in Waldo County in Maine. A superstition exists here that many years ago, valuable treasures were hidden here by pirates at "Cod Lead," which is a gravel mound near the north line of town, directly east of Mosquito Mountain. There are signs of a lot of digging over the years, but so far, without profit. At least, no profit that has been reported. A story of an undisclosed amount of pirate buried treasure is said to be located just above the bridge in Damariscotta, Maine, on the Damariscotta River.

One of the most famous pirates of all time was Captain William or Robert Kidd—historians have written his name both ways. His legend grew more widespread after the death of the pirate, Henry Morgan. People would pick infamous pirates to talk about. Once a pirate died, another pirate was chosen to talk about. It is also a fact that Kidd did indeed visit New England's islands and coast. Rhode Island was a well-known haven for pirates, and Kidd is said to often visit and have dinner with prominent citizens there.

If all the treasure that is credited to Kidd was actually buried, he would not have had time to be a pirate. Still, legends usually have some grain of truth when told, so it is very possible that Kidd did bury some treasure around New England.

Kidd is said to have told about his buried treasure to his jailers, but he was very vague about the actual places. This may have been a ploy to save his life though, or he wanted to be let go before he told anyone where he may have buried his treasure. He was not a foolish man, nor was he considered uneducated.

No one is sure exactly where he may have buried treasure. Only one treasure chest that Kidd is known to have buried was found on Gardiner's Island off the eastern end of Long Island in New York. There could also be a treasure buried on Block Island, Rhode Island, off the eastern end of Long Island Sound.

Right before he was caught, he may have met his wife on the Thimble Islands, perhaps to bury more treasure there since he suspected that he was going to be captured.

He may have buried treasure on Money Island, just off the New Jersey coast, as well. The reason this particular is-land is so interesting is that it is underwater now. The best time to treasure hunt here is on shore after a storm, the time when the ocean sweeps some of its secrets for treasure seekers to discover from the bottom. The island is sunken, but it is located right off the beach, east of Toms River and west of Island Heights. Look for a high eminence on the north shore of Toms River.

Captain Kidd was not a typical pirate captain. He was a meek gentleman of New York City, caught in a web of government intrigue and dying as a scapegoat. He was a victim of the reform movement. Sadly, when he realized that he was a scapegoat, it was too late. He could do nothing to stop the death sentence he was given.

Kidd was a sailor in the merchant service with a wife and family in New York, when the man who may have betrayed him, Sir George or John Bellamont, recruited him. It is said that Kidd was born in 1654 in Dundee, Scotland. His father was a minister, Reverend John Kidd, a Puritan.

Kidd was not a real pirate; he was actually a privateer. Historians have found his "Letter of Marque and Reprisal." On December 11, 1695, the Lord High Admiral of England granted a commission as a private man-of-war to Kidd. He had full power and authority to apprehend, seize, and take into custody, pirates, freebooters, and sea rovers. He, and his crew, would be allowed to take their share of any loot found on these enemy vessels.

Captain Kidd got into so much trouble because a pirate captain is really no one special to the crew, and he had no special rights according to pirate articles. Kidd was honor bound to fire upon other pirate ships and his crew mutinied because of this. Kidd ordered his crew to fire on the pirate ship of Robert Culliford, but Kidd's crew disobeyed. Ninety-five percent of Kidd's crew deserted his ship after this incident. Things started to go quickly downhill after that.

Officially, Kidd was hanged because of a murder he committed. The incident started when the gunner of his crew, William Moore, became the ringleader for the trouble makers on Kidd's ship. Moore was talking to Kidd while sharpening a chisel on the grindstone. Kidd asked Moore why was he causing so much trouble. Moore denied that he was causing any trouble, and that supposedly made Kidd angry. Moore, then, accused Kidd of making him do the things that he did. Kidd seized a wooden bucket that was encircled with iron hoops and smashed it to pieces against Moore's head. The gunner fell onto the deck. He died the next day without ever recovering consciousness. To Kidd, it was punishment for insubordination. To the jury, it was murder.

The last prize that Kidd took was a very rich ship called the *Quedagh Merchant.* This was an Arabian ship that came from the Great Mogul's fleet. He took it in February 1698, and it became Kidd's flag ship. The cargo was large amounts of silk, silver plate, jewels, and gold.

When Kidd was captured, he was taken away in chains to England to be tried. (In 1699, there was no law providing for the trial of pirates in the colonies.)

On February 16, 1700, Kidd was sentenced to be hanged. The East India Company was to take any treasure found from the *Quedagh Merchant,* but not very much was ever found. Kidd was in jail for one year before his trial began, and that is when he told his jailers that he buried the treasure all along the New England coast.

Kidd was convicted for Moore's murder, and on three counts of piracy, in spite of his privateer status. That was simply ignored. On May 23, 1701, Kidd was led to Execution Dock on Wapping-on-the-Thames on the waterfront in London and walked down the pirate stairs to the noose. Kidd had to be hanged twice. The first time, the rope broke and Kidd said that this was an omen of his innocence. The rope was put around his neck the second time, and this time, Kidd died.

After he was declared dead, his body was soaked in tar to preserve it, and suspended in chains to warn other pirates of the price of piracy. Kidd was a victim of circumstances in a political game. Kidd knew that things were looking bad for him, and he was worried, which is one reason why he may have buried treasure before he abandoned the *Quedagh Merchant*.

Why was Kidd so popular? Even after he was hanged, anytime a pirate flag was seen, many believed that it was Kidd. There are two reasons for his popularity. The first is that it is a perfect betrayal story, and the second is that Kidd had a great deal of wealth to be found. He was known to bury treasure; some of it has actually been found. If he buried treasure once, why not more then once? It is known that Kidd had much more loot then was ever discovered.

Perhaps that is the reason for so many claims of his buried treasure. Plus, he did tell his captors that he had buried his wealth, but, as mentioned prior, it could have been a ploy to save his life. The truth may never be known.

In May 1924, some men from Lewiston, Maine were planning to search for Kidd treasure said to be buried along the Sheepscot River. They created a grappling device and they were trying to raise money for the hunt. The story was that when the leader of this group was a child, he was present when the anchor of a sloop on the Sheepscot River hauled in a sea chest. As with many of Kidd's treasures, before it could be brought on board, it broke or fell back into the water. The crew of the sloop was positive that it must have belonged to Kidd. The leader believed that story, so he decided he wanted to search for the lost sea chest. There is no report of any sea chest in the Sheepscot River ever being found.

Dog Mountain in Tremont, Maine in Hancock County is another place that has been thoroughly searched for money hidden by Captain Kidd. Still, nothing has been found there.

Captain Kidd was said to have visited many of the Maine islands in his travels. His treasure is said to be buried on Orrs Island, Bailey's Island, Two Bush Island, Codhead Marsh, Hallowell Island, Pittston Island, Squirrel Island, Isle Au Haut, Monhegan Island, Prospect Island, Stony Brook Island, Heart Island, Jewell Island, and Appledore Island. Some of the claims are interesting and may be true. This book will explore the more credible claims in detail in a future chapter.

Kidd's Hoax Treasure

There is a claim that has been made about Kidd's treasure being buried on Deer Isle that is located in Penobscot Bay, just off the mouth of the Penobscot River in Maine. The problem is that this claim was reported as an amusing hoax the very first time it was declared in 1894. It seems, however, that whenever Kidd's name is mentioned, buried treasure is the only thing that people want to remember. The *Forum Magazine* also printed this story in 1931, and also said that it was not true—just a hoax. Still many people refuse to believe that there is no known Kidd treasure buried on Deer Isle.

The hoax went something like this. In 1890, Franklin H. Head from Chicago visited Frederick Law Olmstead, whose family lived on the island. To amuse his hosts, Head wrote a fictional story that supposedly took place on Deer Isle, called the "Notable Lawsuit."

In summary, the story is about an ancestor of the Olmstead's, about seven generations removed, named Cotton Mather Olmstead, who was a trader from 1696 to 1705 in what would become the state of Maine. He was considered a fair and honest man by the Native Americans he traded with, and the sachem, or chief of the tribe called Winnepasaukee, gave him Deer Isle as a gift. It seems that Olmstead had once saved the life of the chief, when he was attacked by a bear.

So, ever since, part of Deer Isle has remained in the Olmstead family. On the south end of their property is a cave which opens directly to the sea. The cave is about ten feet wide and ten feet high, has an irregular shape, and extends back into the rock formation about twenty-five feet. At high tide, the entire cave is underwater, but at low tide, it is above sea level. It appears that the current Olmstead family visited that cave often at low tide.

On one such visit, Olmstead noticed that there were strange marks on the rocks in the cave. They looked like a cross to him. It was then that he thought the marks may be marking the whereabouts of Kidd's buried treasure. So, the family cleared the floor of the cave, and found a rectangular hole. It looked exactly like what would be left after an iron box was removed. Who could have done that?

The answer soon came. In 1801, Jacques Cartier, an employee of John Jacob Astor, traded with the Maine Native Americans for fur. Oliver Olmstead, the previous owner, apparently sold some of the island to Cartier, but not any of the south end or the cave. Cartier lived on the island with his new wife, and quit his job with the Astor family. Suddenly, he had no money issues, seemed to be well off, and when he drank a bit too much, he would vaguely tell of his good fortune when he arrived on the island. But when he was sober, he would deny what he had said as drunken foolishness.

The people who lived in the area became suspicious, and Cartier suddenly disappeared. Though he tried to destroy papers, some fragments remained, and apparently the papers told of his discovery of the pirate gold in the south cave on Deer Isle. Apparently, Cartier took the iron box and sent it to Astor in New York City.

This is where the lawsuit started.

Olmstead felt that Kidd must have buried his loot in the cave before 1700, after all, he was hanged in 1701. If that were the case, than the loot belonged to Cotton Mather Olmstead, therefore, the Olmstead family. Cartier had stolen the loot from the Olmstead family. After many twists and turns, for over two years, the court determined the following:

1. Kidd sailed along the Maine coast shortly before his arrest and buried an iron box with his initials on Deer Isle. This box was taken from the cave and sent to Mr. Astor.

2. It appeared that Cartier and Astor both became wealthy very quickly after this box was discovered.

3. Astor's wealth seemed to come from selling old Spanish and French gold pieces, some of which may have been part of Kidd's treasure.

However, as is true with many law cases, this case was not ever resolved, and the mystery of Astor's wealth, Olmstead's cave, and Kidd's buried treasure still remains.

So ends the *Notable Lawsuit*, but it was never meant to be published in any way, other than to pass a lazy summer night around a campfire. However, it is a fun treasure tale to tell one more time.

Chapter Four
Blackbeard and His Hidden New England Treasure

Not all the pirates that searched for loot in New England waters were as misunderstood as Kidd. There were pirates that were everything that one thinks a pirate should be. Edward Teach, also known as, Blackbeard, was the typical pirate—hated and feared throughout the area.

He was considered a ranting, raging, and insane pirate. He was the pirate who made men *walk the plank* He buried a lot of treasure, and he committed more private murders then even *he* could count—just because he wanted to.

His origins are unknown and obscure. He was supposedly born in 1690 in Bristol, England, and his last name could be Thatch, Tache, Tatch, Tas, or even Hyde. Historians just could not seem to make up their minds as to what his actual name was. It really did not matter; his reputation made him unforgettable. An orphan and ragamuffin, his early life was almost incomprehensible to what we think about life today. He was even worse off then the poor in England. The poor in the late seventeenth century lived in filth and disease with raw sewage flooding their cellar homes and half the population dying of typhoid, exposure or starvation. Life was said to be worse than that for Blackbeard.

Though it is not known why, somehow, Blackbeard survived. He started his pirate life in his teens, with the pirate,

Benjamin Thornigold, but it did not take him long to learn the trade.

Blackbeard got his nickname because of the black beard that covered his entire face. Totally black, it came up to his eyes, was matted and greasy, and hung down to his chest. He was a dirty and very hairy man. His coat and breeches were usually streaked with food, slime, and blood. He left it that way for effect—and it worked. His hands were the size of barrel tops and were always caked with dirt. He had bat winged, mutilated ears, bulging red-veined eyes, a twisted, broken nose, and raw curling lips. He tied his beard with colored ribbon into small tails, and often tucked it behind his ears. Loud, arrogant, and usually drunk, he was considered a swaggering and merciless brute. He always wore slings over his shoulder that carried three pistols, and his most noted feature was that he had lighted matches under his hat, which appeared on each side of his face, making his eyes look even more wild and fierce. He is said to have fourteen wives before he died.

He was considered the oligarch of the pirate captains in America in his heyday of the early eighteenth century. He had very successful tactics when capturing a ship. In spite of his appearance, he rarely killed the victims or burned the ship, if the crew cooperated completely. However, even the slightest resistance or argument would cause a drastic retaliation from him. For example, if a victim did not voluntarily offer a diamond ring to the pirate, then Blackbeard would cut off the victim's finger.

Blackbeard was also mostly civil to other pirates, but he never considered them equal to him. He was a tyrant on his ship, but the crew did not vote him out, because he brought in so many rich prizes. He had a marksman eye, and the ability to succeed in a dirty fight. His thirst for blood was said to be unmatched by any pirate at that time.

When Blackbeard decided to be a captain on his own, it only took him a few months to become one of the most feared and despised pirates in America. His flag ship was called the *Queen Anne's Revenge*. He usually had a three- or four-ship squadron when he cruised. His pirate flag was black, with a white skeleton stabbing a red heart, which signified blood. When his crew had shore leave, everyone in the town hoped he had enough loot, until he left. It was said that as his money thinned, his disposition soured.

There is no doubt that Blackbeard was a hated, feared pirat. The proof of this was the hundred-pound bounty for the head of the dreaded pirate. Blackbeard gave his crew very good advice for staying alive, "Keep moving." He did not take his own advice, and it was his own downfall. He died of twenty-five wounds, five were caused by pistol, and a cutlass caused the rest. The fight lasted only ten minutes, but it is said that it was a horrifying fight.

The end for Blackbeard started in November 1718, when the *HMS Pearl* crew managed to board Blackbeard's ship at Ocrancoke Islet, and Lt. Maynard be-headed him. Even as Blackbeard stiffened and died, he fell forward, and his cutlass nearly cut off Maynard's foot. Blackbeard's body was thrown overboard, but his head was hung on the bow sprit of the ship as a trophy. All of his crew were executed.

Not too long before Blackbeard was killed, a crew member supposedly asked him where he had buried all his treasure.

His answer was, "Nobody but the devil and myself know where my treasure is and the longer liver of the two shall have it."

Blackbeard has supposedly buried treasure on a few of Maine's islands. Legends state that an immense treasure of gold ingots is buried by this pirate on Smuttynose Island in the Isles of Shoals just off the coast. This, and other Blackbeard treasures, as well as the ghosts that guard his loot, are buried at other places on the Isles of Shoals. That entire story will also be told in a later chapter.

Chapter Five
Edward Low, the Hated New England Pirate

One of the most disliked pirates that ever roamed the New England coast, and one who seemed to love to torment the New England people, was Edward Low or Lowe. He was also known as the most villainous Ned Low. For some reason, he prowled New England and loved to torture anyone he captured from that area. He was not well-liked by the people who lived in the area, and perhaps he did not like being shunned, so he decided to punish anyone who came from New England. In fact, it was said that he saved his worse tortures for the people of New England and Portugal. Low was the pirate who gave the pirate lore the cruel-nature persona. It was said that he had a split personality; he could be terribly cruel one minute, and the next minute, he could be extremely hospitable to others.

There is a story about Low finding three fishermen from the Isles of Shoals, just off the Maine and New Hampshire coast. He threatened to kill them, unless they jumped up and down and cursed the Reverend Cotton Mather three times. (It is a known fact that the pirates detested Mather, because he was fond of preaching long funeral sermons to condemned pirates, as they were about to be hanged.) The fact that is not clear is why Low bothered with the fisherman in the first place. They had no treasure to plunder, so it could be surmised that he just liked to torment people. The second question that comes to mind, is why it would even matter if they cursed Mather—it seemed as though Low was just out having fun tormenting people.

By trade, Low was a sail maker in Boston before he became a master and wicked pirate. He saved the most vile cruelties he could think of for captured crews, but was considered nasty, cruel, and mean to all, even his own crew. It was said that he would plunder a shipwreck vessel, and instead of killing the crew, he would just leave them to die on the floundering ship. If he thought there would be any type of resistance, he would not usually attack a vessel. Rather, basically, he would go after the weak and defenseless ships. However, there are also legends in New England that Low cut off the captured Captain's lips and ears for sport.

Low was born in Westminster, England, and even at a young age, he always wanted to be a thief. He was known as a land pirate at a very young age. When he decided to become a sea pirate, he started with a small vessel and a dozen unarmed men, but he quickly became head of the largest piratical force in American waters. One particular quirk that Low had was that he would only take unmarried men on as his crew. No one is really sure why, but there is a story that Low's wife in Boston died shortly before he became a pirate in New England. It is also said that he was fond of his small child left behind. Some say that he would even weep at times, when he thought about her death and his child.

One interesting fact about Low was that his pirate flag was different than most. He had a blue cloth, with a black design of his own making, displaying a red skeleton in the middle.

Low had a diabolical leer because of an accident. Legend states that a crewmember's cutlass that was cutting at someone else, missed, and hit Low's face. The ship's doctor, after drinking a lot, sewed him up, but Low complained to the doctor, so the doctor is said to have hit him, knocking the stitches out. The cut healed, but the resulting scar was horrible to look at.

Low is supposed to have buried treasure in the eighteenth century, on Pond Island, in the Casco Bay area of Maine, near Popham Beach, which he took from the Spanish Galleon, *Don Pedro del Montdova*. The Spanish treasure ship reached the Florida Keys and was chased by a British Gunboat. The Spanish ship went off course and managed to outrun the gunboat. The captain of the treasure ship decided to hide out in Casco Bay, until it was safe to head for Spain. He had no idea that Low was also hiding out in Casco Bay, and Low quickly captured the ship and treasure. Low tortured the captain until he found out where the treasure was hidden on the ship and then he killed the crew. He decided to sink the ship, after taking the treasure, of course, because he knew that the British gunboat was still looking for the *Don Pedro*.

The treasure consisted of three kettles of bar silver and a large wooden chest full of gold and jewels. According to legend, ten pirates and three boats were needed to carry the treasure to the island. Low is said to have dropped the loot into the middle of the freshwater pond in the center of Pond Island, which is one of the Harpswell area islands. The island is named for this pond. Low knew that the pond was there because he had been to the island before to fill his water casks. They quickly left the island, and it was at that time that the

British ships gave chase, but Low outran them, and headed toward the Caribbean.

Many years passed before anyone even knew of the treasure that was said to be buried on Pond Island. While dying, one of Low's mates finally told the story, when he realized that he would not be able to retrieve the treasure himself.

As many buried treasure stories go, there are also two dead pirates who were killed on the spot to guard the treasure. Visitors and residents have reported seeing strange red lights on the island, and the muffled angry voices of quarreling pirates have been heard. Perhaps the voices were treasure hunters looking for the treasure and not being very successful. There have been at least one hundred documented expeditions searching for this treasure, but no reports of discovering the loot. Perhaps the ghostly guards are successfully hiding the spot.

The facts are that Low was preying on the northern shipping lanes in this area around 1726, so perhaps there is more to this story then one would think. The pond area has been drained and searched, but heavy items tend to sink in mud. The treasure could be buried very deep by now. It is said now that a treasure seeker can not get to the treasure because Low killed two of his crew, who still guard the loot. People claim to hear moans and groans, as well as yelling. Today the treasure has become enchanted and it is said that it will never be found, which is the reason that people are killed to guard the treasure in the first place.

There is documentation of a person who died on this island. John Darling was a man who was causing problems in Harpswell, Maine, and was exiled to Pond Island. He lived there alone for twenty years. Duck hunters found him one winter dead, frozen as hard as a stone.

Harpswell Treasures

The Harpswell area is made up of forty-seven offshore islands—most are located in Maine. Local lore suggests that the islands are haunted or cursed, and legends abound in this area about the pirate, who buried treasure on the islands. But those stories are vague in details.

There may be *something* to these stories, though. Farmers in this area had excellent luck in finding treasure there. On Haskill Island, a farmer who was plowing his field, found a pot of gold worth about eighteen hundred dollars, during the Civil War. In Harpswell Center, another farmer, who was again plowing a field, found one thousand, one hundred dollars in gold.

Harpswell Neck is a peninsula about a mile in length, which extends southward. The Native Americans in the area called it Merryconeag. It is said that an unhappy phantom ship appears and disappears periodically along the shore. It seems to come close to shore, and then drifts back to the sea. The legend states that the ship is of ancient build with tall masts and sails, but the name, port of origin, and flag are missing. Like the *Dash*, this ship appears to be a bad omen to the person who observes the ship.

The only silver ever found on the island was by the Acaraza Man. In 1801, a stranger came to the island, who claimed that he could extract silver from dew. Not surprisingly, his first attempt at this phenomena failed, but his second attempt did manage to extract silver. He said that it was because the dew was "collected at the right time of the morning" the second time. When the brew he was mixing cooled, silver particles were found in the bottom of the container. The group of men, who were financing him, paid the stranger for his formula, and the stranger, who was obviously a con artist, disappeared. Of course, the formula never worked again.

Garnet caves are said to exist on these islands. Garnet is said to be the only light that illuminated Noah's Ark. Large garnet crystals are not uncommon in Maine. Garnet is a translucent, deep red mineral that is found in metamorphic rock and pegmatites. The garnet is associated with strong sexual potency and believed to protect the wearer against the effects of poison, cure depression, and protect against bad dreams. The mineral is found in all colors, except blue. (As an interesting side note, there is a known garnet site in the Casco Bay area near Bath on Hermit Island near Small Point. Perhaps it is not such a leap of faith to believe that these garnet caves do exist, and can be found today.)

Low's Ultimate End

Pond Island is the only island where Low is said to have buried treasure, though there is a story that when Low robbed the very rich Portugal ship, *Nostra Signinora de Victoia*, he did not bury it on Pond Island, but actually buried it somewhere else in Sagadohoc County, Maine, though the details are vague. The legend states that this treasure was buried along the road from Maine to Canada in Sagadohoc County. Perhaps he did not bury all the loot on the island, and decided to bury some of it elsewhere.

Officially, on June 10, 1723, Captain Peter Sogard of the *HMS Greyhound*, a British Man-Of-War, was looking for Low and found him. Low had two ships, his flag ship called *Fancy* where he was captain and his consort ship, called *Ranger*; captained by Charles Harris. Low deserted the *Ranger* and that ship was captured, but Low managed to escape on the *Fancy*. Twenty-five to twenty-seven of his men were hanged for piracy at Newport, Rhode Island.

No one really knows what happened to Low after his disappearance from the Maine coast. It is said that his luck finally ran out. He continued to plunder ships, but was caught. His trial was brief, he was convicted, and hanged, before ever returning to Maine. It is also said that he died of yellow fever in New Orleans. Others say that his crew mutinied when Low killed his quartermaster in a fit of anger, so they set him adrift, and when he was picked up by a French Warship, he was taken to Martinique to be hanged. Still another tale advises that Low went to Brazil or that his new ship called *Merry Christmas* was wrecked with all hands lost.

Whatever happened to Low, it is probably safe to say that not too many New England natives were sorry that he prowled their waters no more.

Chapter Six
John Quelch, the Arrogant New England Pirate

John Quelch was the suave pirate that one would think of as a swashbuckler. He was arrogant, confident, and never believed anything bad could ever happen to him. That probably was his undoing. Quelch considered himself a privateer, not a pirate, though he did not have any documents to prove that the government sanctioned his plundering, and he never gave any percentage of his taken loot to the government.

He was described as villainous, despicable, and a murderous man. His pirate flag was a black square, and in the middle was a skeleton holding a hourglass in one hand, and in the other hand was a dart with three drops of blood dripping from it. He was more feared in the Atlantic, then anywhere else in the world.

Quelch had very good luck, and there were rich prizes on the ships that he took. He never had any witnesses to his crimes, because he always killed all the crew on the captured ships.

In May 1704, Quelch anchored his ship, *Charles*, off the coast of Marblehead, Massachusetts, and decided to go on shore leave. He was considered a pirate by then, so the fact that he went to Massachusetts, and just walked on shore tells the story of how confident he was that nothing bad would ever happen to him. He actually believed he was blameless and thought he could talk himself out of any situation. He always considered himself a pretty good liar.

Quelch had an amazing story to tell the authorities. He told them that the rightful owner of the *Charles* had died at sea and had begged Quelch to take command. Quelch said that all the booty that they had was actually taken from a wrecked Spanish ship. Unfortunately for Quelch, the tobacco, salt, sugar, and flour found on his ship would not have been found on a Spanish treasure wreck.

What Quelch did not realize was that, though he never left any of his victims alive to give him up (after all dead men tell no tales), he *did* let his own crew go on shore. Members of his crew got drunk, and told anyone who would listen what really happened on the *Charles*. They described how Quelch fired on the ship and killed all the crew by throwing them overboard.

When Quelch was told what was said, he said that he did not kill the captain of the *Charles*, but just did not object when his crew did what they did. This was why Quelch was convicted of piracy. He practically gave himself to the authorities.

No one really gave credit to his claims of being a privateer, not a pirate. It is a fact that he murdered people and stole their goods. Quelch pled innocent at his trial, and stated that he was paid by the merchants of Boston to do what he did. Perhaps he *was* paid to do what he did; no one knows for sure.

Six of his crew were hanged, including Quelch, by forty soldiers on June 13, 1704. The gallows were set on Brough-ton's Hill, where Copp's Hill Cemetery is today, between the rise and fall of the tide, either on Bird's Island or Nix's Mate Island. Both of these islands are now underwater, and no longer exist in Boston Harbor.

After Quelch died, he was strung up on chains to warn other pirates of what would happen if they continued to plunder and were caught. Quelch's last statement was this, "I am not afraid of the gallows. I am not afraid of death. I desire to know what I am here for. I am condemned only upon circumstances." At this time, an unknown person in the audience spoke up, probably lambasting the many supposed "non-pirates" who got rich with pirate ways. "You should also beware of bringing money into New England to be hanged for it."

Quelch visited a few islands off New England before he sailed into Marblehead on that fateful summer day. His loot from the *Charles* was supposedly one hundred weight of gold dust, thousands of gold and silver coins, silks, and taffeta. When the *Charles* was boarded, all that was ever found was forty-two ounces of gold dust. The treasure on board estimated to have been about $275,000. It was concluded that Quelch must have buried the rest in some other location.

It has been said that Quelch could have buried the loot on Snake Island, near Cape Ann in Massachusetts, or perhaps he buried it on one of the Isles of Shoals, either Appledore or on Star Island. At this point, Star Island seems to be the better choice. It is said that Quelch hid a large amount of Portuguese plunder there, supposedly just for a while.

It is also possible that Quelch buried the rest of his *Charles* loot on Star Island, just to keep it safe, while he tried to pull a fast one on the authorities in Boston.

The real questions are: Why did Quelch think he could lie his way out of the murder, or did he really think he could not be caught? Did he do it just for the thrill of it? No one knows, but one fact is sure, Quelch died with a lot of loot hidden somewhere.

Chapter Seven
Samuel Bellamy's New England Kingdom

The pirate, Samuel Bellamy, was considered blood thirsty and villainous, and considered gold his personal God. Believe it or not, he was also considered the "Robin Hood of the High Seas." Perhaps, the man may not have been as horrible as his reputation has been portrayed. He did not always murder the victims of plundered ships; he offered them the opportunity to join his crew, if they would become Communists. If the victim crew refused to join him, he still would not kill them; he would just sail away and leave them to the mercy of the sea—after disabling their ship. He figured the sea would kill them, and he would be considered innocent of murder.

It is said that Bellamy once claimed to the captain of a captured ship. "I am a free prince and I have as much authority to make war on the whole world, as he who has one hundred sails of ships at sea and an army of one hundred thousand men in the field, and this is what my conscience tells me. Those who will submit to be governed by laws which rich men have made for their own security, for the cowardly whelps have not the courage to otherwise defend what they got by their knavery."

Like many of the other pirates of the era, Bellamy was from England, with bushy black hair, a square cut black beard and piercing black eyes, which is why he received his nickname of Black Bellamy or the Black Prince.

Bellamy was actually a salvager by trade, until a pirate ship captured him. He was in the process of salvaging a Spanish treasure ship, when two pirate ships seized him and took his salvaged loot. Bellamy joined the pirate ship to get a piece of his own salvaged treasure. The ship was called the *Mary Ann*, captained by Ben Horingold. After a while, the crew voted Horingold out, and voted for Bellamy to become their captain.

Bellamy did not let his crew down. He immediately seized a three-masted French Galley, called by a variety of names. Historians have called it the *Whidaw, Whydah, Widdah* or *Whidah*. Captain Prince, the former captain of the *Whydah*, did not show any resistance to the takeover, and Bellamy gave him and any crewmember that did not covert and join him, twenty pounds of silver and gold. That was how much treasure was found on this ship. He could give pounds of gold and silver away to the victim crew, without his crew caring too much.

Bellamy captured the *Whydah* on January 9, 1717, and it was said to be carrying twenty thousand pounds of gold and silver coins or $20,000, and $100,000 in bullion from only one of the chests in the Captain's quarters. The rest of the cargo was indigo, elephant teeth, gold dust, and sugar. Legend states that there were one hundred crewmembers on board Bellamy's ship, and their cut of this haul was a bag that weighed fifty pounds each.

It is said that Bellamy and his crew took the *Whydah* to a land where there were no others around, with plenty of fresh water in the river for sailing for almost two miles. Bellamy called this land, Machisas, and he decided to settle there and build a fort. Today the area is called Machias, Maine and it is near the present bridge on Route 1. Under this fort, the pirates constructed an underground vault for storing their loot. He wanted to name his new town, Norumbega, after the ancient city of gold that was said to exist in this area and hoped it would become a center of a pirate empire.

Bellamy's fort was built with thick heavy logs that were surrounded by a moat and earthen walls. The fort was built on both sides of the Machias River, exactly where Highway 1-A crosses the river in Machias Township and supposedly has an underground vault with pounds of stolen loot inside. Bellamy's friend, Paulsgrave Williams, is said to have helped Bellamy build this vault in 1716, stating that it was dug to a great depth, lined with flagstone and roofed with heavy oak beams. Many chests and bags that contained gold and silver bars, coins, weapons, and jewels were placed in the vault. Spanish American coins and Massachusetts silver were thought to be part of this treasure. The treasure is said to be one hundred and eighty bags of gold, each weighing fifty pounds. There are also gold ingots, silver coins, gems and ivory.

As usual, crewmembers were killed after building the vault to guard the treasure and to keep the secret of what was there. After caught, the crew that remained alive, swore that Bellamy never divided the loot with them. Fifteen to thirty million dollars supposedly lies at least fifteen feet below the surface. The treasure may lie deeper today because of cave-ins and earthquakes. It is also said that he left a two or three million dollar treasure near the mouth of the Machias River.

The mouth of the river has many irregular mounds and hollows that, at first glance, appear to be natural irregularities of the land—but are they really sites of pirate holdings? It is a remote area even today, so it is no surprise that Bellamy wanted to stay there, and preach his Communist views in this beautiful area.

Bellamy decided that the Machias Bay area in Maine would be his pirate kingdom, like the kingdom in Madagascar. He did not want to spend his life on the run and intended to make the Machias area his monarchy. He would live here and send out ships on plundering expeditions when his funds ran low.

Bellamy was not the first pirate to use the Machias area, which is a Native American word meaning "little bad river," as a pirate base of operations. The pirate Rhodes supposedly used this locale in the early 1700s for a pirate base before Bellamy arrived. The location seemed to serve well as a hiding place for pirates. It was screened from observation from the sea by islands and the winding approach, and there was plenty of fresh water. Life was beginning to flourish here for the band of pirates.

After a while, however, Bellamy's men decided that if they were going to live in this place, they needed the companionship of women. They obviously did not want to just pirate the coast for Bellamy who would stay on land; they wanted to bring women to live in their new community. They must have had an extensive amount of loot to start thinking about settling down. So, the crew left on the *Whydah* one more time, not to pirate, but to find women to settle in Maine.

Bellamy and his crew may have intended to return to their settled lives, but the French were not so forgiving or willing to forget what Bellamy had stolen from them over time. As soon as they saw the *Whydah*, they attacked. Bellamy lost half his crew quickly and he left the area and sailed into Cape Cod.

Samuel Bellamy, the one time salvager, would now sail into history. With only half his crew, the *Whydah* was difficult to control. It is ironic that this ship was destined to become one of the most famous wrecks to be salvaged of all time.

On April 26, 1717, things started to go very wrong on the *Whydah*. The day started with a heavy fog, and was followed by nasty thunderstorms. By 10:00 pm, the crew that was left was drinking heavily. The Madeira wine they had brought with them was almost gone. The drinking crew and dangerous storms caused the *Whydah* to veer way off course. The anchors failed to hold against the breakers. The *Whydah* crashed against a sand bar off the shore with terrible force, capsizing at once. One hundred and forty six crewmembers were thrown into the sea and all except two drowned. It is considered Cape Cod's first great shipwreck. The ship was wrecked off Wellfleet, Massachusetts and recovered in modern times about two miles south of the life saving station and about twelve miles north of Orleans.

The two crewmembers who escaped the sinking of the *Whydah* were the ship's carpenter and a seaman. Both were acquitted of being pirates because they said that they did not want to become pirates, but Bellamy had forced them. It was a well-known fact, at the time, that Bellamy did indeed force men to join him, or they were stranded and left to die.

In 1984, Barry Clifford of Maritime Explorations salvaged the *Whydah* for a cost of six million dollars. The ship was found in twenty-five feet of water. The group found eight thousand coins, dueling pistols made of Black Walnut, silk socks, the ship's bell, cannons, and sailor clay pipes. That was it. It is known that Bellamy had much more treasure, and it was not all spent in Machias. There was nothing to spend it on in that area at the time. Therefore, the rest of his treasure must be somewhere else.

As an interesting side note to this fascinating story, it is also said that Bellamy buried some of his treasure on Deer Isle. This is the same Deer Isle as Kidd's treasure hoax story. Perhaps there is more to this island than one may believe. Over $1,500,000 has been found on this island, but it is still believed that more of Bellamy's, as well as other pirates' treasure, still exists there.

Wherever Bellamy left his treasure, it is sure that the *Whydah* was not carrying his full loot when it sank in 1717.

Chapter Eight
Dixey Bull:
New England's First Pirate

Dixey Bull or Dixie Bull—historians spell this pirate's name differently—was the first pirate to cruise the North American coast. He was a beaver fur trader from northern Maine, but was believed to be of English descent. The change from fur trader to pirate was made in June 1632. Bull lost his Shallop vessel and cargo to a band of French renegades. He set out to plunder the French for revenge, but found that he liked the pirate life. It was very lucrative and very easy money. Bull decided to start robbing his fellow colonial traders, instead of trapping for the fur himself. He was not well-liked, and was well-known from Mount Desert Island to the shores of the Piscataqua River in Maine for his pirate ways. The first United States naval demonstration in the British colonies was against Dixie Bull.

Penobscot Bay was one of Bull's favorite trading spots when he was a fur trader. And it proved just as a great place for pirating. He prowled the Pemaquid, Maine area for two years, and then set his sights on Richmond Island off the coast of Maine. Supposedly, he was said to mistreat everyone and anyone he met.

Dixie was mentioned in the land grant of York, Maine, and was called a man of adventurous disposition by the man that probably sent him to the Americas, Sir Fernando Gorges.

Dixie had a fifteen-man crew, and on his first seized ship, he took over five hundred pounds (English currency). Dixie escaped many times because of the unpredictable Maine weather, but his good luck would not last forever. In 1633, one lucky shot by a victim crew member killed his first in command. Dixie and his crew managed to escape, but the death caused his crew to be very upset and in shock. None of them had ever seen bloodshed like that before.

Dixie and his crew soon left American waters and never returned. It was rumored that the entire crew went to Europe. What really happened to Bull is unknown. Reports say (according to a popular poem in the 1600s) that he was killed in a sword fight. That just may have been wishful thinking at the time.

There are two islands where Dixie supposedly left a treasure legacy behind. The first island is Cushing Island. It has also been called Portland Island, Andrews Island, Fort Island, Bangs Island, and Andross Island. Dixie was believed to have visited this island and buried a treasure, but how much he buried is unknown. The legend states that a storm came up suddenly with very high winds, just as his ship was entering the channel between South Portland and Cushing Island, so Dixie went to shore to wait out the storm. While he was there, it is said that he decided to bury some of his treasure for safekeeping.

The other island where Bull supposedly left treasure was Damariscove Island. This was an early landfall place for Europeans. The island has a great harbor of fifteen hundred feet at high tide, then ten to fifteen feet at low tide, and usually very calm. Dixie visited this island also, and is said to have buried $400,000.

It is a very good place to bury a treasure. Damariscove Island is located in the south end of Boothbay Harbor, and it is now deserted. There is a supernatural history associated with this island. It is said that this is the island where the Europeans first visited America. The fishermen were using it to salt the fish they caught. The ghost of Captain Richard Pattishall is said to still be here, guarding whatever treasure that was left behind, even if he did not actually bury the loot himself. He was be-headed and tossed into the bay by the Native Americans in 1689. His body, and that of his dog (who jumped in behind him), washed up in this location. The island is owned and protected by the Nature Conservancy today.

Dixie was also said to have visited Haskell Island in Casco Bay, Maine, where he may have buried some other plunder. That story will come later in the islands of Casco Bay chapter.

Though no one is sure what happened to Dixie, it can be surmised that Dixie began some of the traits that the pirates who came after him are well-known for. Though not much is known about this man, he does have the dubious honor of being considered the first North American pirate.

Chapter Nine

New England's Island Pirate Buried Treasures

There are fifteen places where *X* does mark the spot in Maine and there have been maps made or treasure found to supposedly prove this fact. These places are the ones that supposedly show where the treasure or lost mine is buried. Beware, however, if you search for these treasures, because they are also haunted. The buried treasure buried on these islands are guarded by murdered pirate crew members or their slaves.

Peddler Woes

The first tale is not about pirate treasure, but of treasure stolen and accompanied by murder—and perhaps still being protected by the victim. Peddlers who sold their wares in Maine seemed to disappear rather mysteriously in earlier times. It was certainly one of the more dangerous jobs to have in an earlier era. The first peddler story starts in 1840. Mother York owned a home at 304 Main Street in Springvale, Maine. She was not known in the area as a strange person, but two men regularly visited her, and there was speculation as to the reason why. Mother York was a quiet person, who kept to herself, but the gossip as to what was going on never stopped.

One day, a peddler came to town with his wares and visited Mother York's house. His cart was filled with beautiful lace, gold and silver jewelry, colorful silks, cigars, and anything else that he could sell. The peddler and his cart disappeared in the night, and he was never seen or heard from again. During that same night, Mother York and her two companions also disappeared, and were never heard from again.

It was claimed that the peddler's cart was seen leaving town that night with Mother York and her two friends driving furiously toward Canada, but that was never proven. It was speculated that Mother York and the two strangers murdered the peddler and left the area with the stolen goods. However, the stolen goods were never spent.

The house remained abandoned for a long time. When it was finally rented or sold, the new residents always complained of strange sounds and sights that would come from inside the house. They claimed that they heard corn being husked in the attic, they would see pot lids on the stove rising to remain suspended in mid-air, there were footsteps on the stairs, and the slamming of doors and windows were constant when no one was around.

So well-known is this legend that in 1871, when a reporter stayed in the house and reported that nothing happened, no one believed his article. The house was eventually torn down in the early 1970s, and it is hoped that the peddler finally is at peace, though it is thought that perhaps some of the peddler's goods are still buried around there.

Peddler Pond

Peddler's treasure is also said to be in the Rangeley Lake area, around a group of small ponds that are called the Sandy

River Ponds. One of these ponds is called Peddler Pond, because of an unsolved murder that supposedly took place near there in the 1830s.

Traveling in that time was difficult at best. To move from one place to another, especially over land in rural Maine, was not an easy task. The people that did travel from Farmington to Rangeley often had to stop at the Half-Way House for the evening. This place was called the Half-Way House because it was halfway between Madrid and Rangeley. By the time the horses got here, either by stage or a single rider, they were exhausted, and needed to be watered, fed, and put to rest for the night.

The Half-Way House was close to a small pond that was one of the Sandy River Ponds group. This inn was owned by a person who would tend to over-charge his guests. More often than not, he would also charge for the grain for the horses, but he would seldom give the horses that grain. He got away with this type of business because he owned the only place in the area that could accommodate overnight guests.

One night, a peddler with a two-wheeled push cart stopped for the night. After being wined and dined, the peddler started to unload his cart. He showed the owner of the Half-Way House the wares he was to sell the next day in Rangeley. He unloaded watches, fine clothing, jewelry, mirrors, handkerchiefs, shawls, and other fancy goods, under the watchful eye of the inn's owner.

The House guests retired for the night, and by the next morning, the peddler and his push cart had disappeared. There was no sign of him then, or ever since. He completely disappeared forever. The hired man said there were no push cart tracks in the dust on the road in the morning, and he made it clear that he believed that his boss had murdered the peddler, stole all his goods, and hid them. He thought that his boss had tied the peddler's body to his push cart, which was then loaded onto a raft and sunk in the middle of the small pond near his establishment. There was no evidence, or even a body, to prove anything, so no charges were ever brought against the owner, but it is a good bet that the hired man no longer worked there after his allegations.

Shortly after this time, the owner enlisted in the army, and was gone from the area for thirteen years. When he did return, he was supposedly looking for gold in the foothills of Saddleback Mountain.

Memories tend to last a long time in the rural parts of the country. One day, the owner was seen by a trapper, exiting a cave, and carrying what looked like a heavy backpack. The previous owner of the Half-Way House looked around, but apparently did not notice the trapper, dropped the backpack in the heavy thicket, and started back toward town. The trapper caught up with the owner, and engaged in small conversation, but the owner never mentioned the pack, so the trapper became suspicious.

When they reached town, they parted ways, and the trapper immediately went to the authorities with his story. It was suspected that the owner may have been retrieving his stolen goods, or some of the goods, from the murdered peddler. There is no statute of limitations for murder, so a posse was immediately formed to search for the owner and the backpack.

No trace of the owner or the pack was ever found. The owner, like the peddler, was never seen again. The pond was never dragged, and no sign of any of the peddler's wares has ever turned up. Perhaps on the bottom of the muddy pond lies the answer, or perhaps the peddler finally found justice. Whatever happened, the peddler's goods are still missing or hidden somewhere.

Cursed Coin

There are also cursed treasures that have been discovered in Maine. This is the story about a treasure that only brings bad luck to those who find it. Sandy Duguid was a fisherman who once found a pirate treasure at Norton's Point in Penobscot Bay, Maine, in Washington County in the early nineteenth century. The legend goes that one day he found three cairns of rocks that formed a triangle. Like every other treasure hunter, he knew that this could only mean that a pirate treasure was buried nearby. He immediately started digging and found a flat rock. Under that rock, was a wooden chest filled with Spanish gold and silver. At this point, a seeker would normally consider himself very lucky, and Sandy did, indeed, consider himself very lucky.

This was not the case, however. There was a curse with this treasure, and the message he found in the chest read, "A curse on the man who removes this chest and upon the region. Let him beware. Misfortune will follow him to the end of his days."

Duguid ignored this warning; there was too much money at stake. But in the days to follow, things started to happen. There was blight on his crops, he could no longer catch any fish, illness came to his family, and finally, lightning struck his home, burning it to the ground. This fisherman never had good luck again. No one really knows what happened to Sandy. He just disappeared from the records.

Years later, Patrick Collins built a house where Sandy had once lived. While he was building the home, he found an ancient Spanish coin. He could not believe his good luck. One day, when he was on his way home from work, he passed a working quarry where dynamite had just been set. As it exploded, a piece of the dynamite hit his leg, and the leg had to be amputated.

A friend of Patrick's borrowed the coin to study it. As he passed the same quarry to get to Patrick's home, another blast occurred, this time blinding his friend. Still another friend was thought to borrow this coin, and he went crazy. The coin is said to have disappeared.

Think that is the end of this haunted treasure tale? Think again, because many years later, a college professor got the same coin for a museum. The ship he was sailing on suddenly sank, and this time the coin disappeared under the waves. Perhaps that would finally end the curse on the coin and the treasure—at least for now.

Island Treasures

There are six treasure spots in Cumberland County, Maine. They are Jewell Island, Great Chebeaque Island, Richmond Island, Cushing Island, Johns Island and Gott Island. The three spots in Hancock County, Maine are Oak Island, Two Bush Island and Codhead Marsh. In Lincoln County, Maine, the two places are Outer Heron Island and Alma Island. In Waldo County, Maine there is only one treasure spot on Stony Brook Island. There will be more treasure hunting informa-

tion on these islands further in the book. The last two treasure islands in Maine are found in York County on the Isles
of Shoals islands, Smuttynose and Appledore. There are also
stories of golden hoards buried by the French colonists that
lived on Fernald's Point on Mount Desert Island.

An interesting side note to the island treasure stories is
that some of the islands have changed names, so perhaps
there are more or less of the actual islands that have treasure
buried on them. The maps also have landmarks on them that
are long gone, and there is no way to know where they may
have been at the time the treasure was buried there.

Why does Maine have so many islands where treasure is
rumored to be buried? This island building process began
when the glacier capping the North Pole started to expand,
and it crept right over northern New England. The thickness
of this ice was incredible. At the edge, where it was the most
thin, it was 1,000 feet deep. The weight of this ice literally
crushed the land causing it to sink, and much of the land that
we live on today was literally under the ocean.

The reason that northern New England has so many
lakes, streams, brooks, and rivers is because of the ice cap
that covered it for so many years. The coast was also created
by this ice and it is considered one of the most irregular and
rugged in the world.

Geologists state that Maine is considered a drowned coastline. That means that the coast was much higher in prehistoric
times. When the ice finally receded, the land rose just a bit, but
the Maine coast is very long and ragged, dotted with islands,
which are mountaintops coming out of the ocean. Geologists
say that the islands were once the high spots of hilly regions,

and depressed during the glacial period. Though islands regained some of their mass, the coast never regained all of it, so the islands seen today were born. Hence, all Maine islands are continental islands, meaning that all were once part of the mainland.

These islands even have a place in the discussion over who really discovered America first. Though it has been argued that Vikings may have been the first people to discover North America and New England, it can also be argued that the first people to find North America came from Asia, following the game trails. It is thought that it may have taken only nine hundred years to make it from the west coast to New England, once these prehistoric people crossed the Bering Straits. It is from these stone age people that Maine's mysterious Red Paint People may have come from.

Grand Pre Tale

Following the ancient trails and roads is one way to search for lost treasure, especially in northern New England. One example of this is the trail taken by the settlers of Grand Pre in Aroostook County, Maine. Grand Pre Village was completely captured one dark and foggy night, so the story starts. The British decided that the Acadians would have to leave this area and return to France. They marched all the people from the village, after killing all their livestock and burning all their homes, of course, to the shore to board a number of ships to leave Maine forever.

On one ship, twelve Acadian fishermen were on deck and grew more angry as the ship left shore. The officer on deck became rather nervous at the excited, foreign language that these men were speaking, and ordered them below decks. The men refused, they wanted to watch their home shoreline for as long as they could. The officer could not understand what they were asking, so he drew his sword. The fishermen just grew more angry.

They rebelled and a struggle ensued. The British soldiers were surprised by the attack and outnumbered by the people who were on board. They were quickly overpowered. A French fisherman quickly took the wheel of the ship, and turned the boat back toward shore.

They headed into the St. John River, but the ship went aground about thirty miles above Fredericton. The rebels stripped the boat of anything they could carry, and left the British to fend for themselves.

The Acadians settled about six miles from the river. It was the winter of 1755, and it happened to be an especially harsh and brutal winter. Many of the settlers died there. The Native Americans living in the area did help the Grand Pre survivors live through the brutal cold as much as possible. The good news was that the harsh conditions kept the British from searching for them.

A young priest of the group decided that he would lead them out of danger and far away from the British. The St. John River was the only avenue for escape. Boats were found, fixed, or stolen, and as soon as spring arrived in the valley, they left. They did not have room for all they had taken earlier, so at this point, there were three areas where everything that they needed to leave behind could be hidden—the Grand Pre Village, the aground ship on the St. John River, and the make-shift winter residence.

It was a very difficult river journey. The water was high that spring because of the huge snow melt and the current was extremely strong. Many items had to be left all along the river. One day, thunder was heard in the distance, but it was a low rumbling that never stopped all day. That night, at the camp, Native Americans told the fleeing villagers that the sound was the leaping river down the walls of a mountain, also known as a waterfall. The travelers would travel no further, they reached Woolastook Falls. The spot they chose was four miles above these falls. Hamlin Plantation became their new home in May 1756. Whenever a treasure seeker hears a story about people fleeing or being forced from their homes, the entire route becomes a map of where treasure may have been hidden or lost.

The above story is just one treasure legend that abounds in Aroostook County. In Maine, this large area is simply known as "The County." All along the St. John River and Allagash River, the treasure seeker could find many logging era relics. These were well traveled rivers during the logging days. There were also many deaths on the river during that time, and supernatural legends have existed there since the first Native American settled in the area. This region was created by violent forces on Earth; it is no wonder that certain places there are truly enchanted.

Allagash Logging Legend

One logging story starts on the Allagash River and Allagash Falls. This fall site is located on the Allagash River in Township 15, Range 11. The word Allagash is Abenaki, means "bark cabin." These falls have a thirty to forty foot drop, right where the St. John and Allagash Rivers meet. Large boulders in the stream bed cause violent, turbulent rapids.

There are many legends about this place such as the appearance of an old Native American man, whose face appears in the rock beneath the falls. There is also a Native American maiden, who threw herself off the ledge of the falls. She appears at the top of these falls to people who may be getting too close to the edge of the drop.

This place is only accessible by canoe, and is a portage, which is a place where canoes are carried past the raging river. This is part of the geological Seboomook Formation. It was created over four hundred million years ago, when the ocean covered most of northern Maine. There were massive young mountains here, and volcanoes were spewing lava all over the area. Ocean currents deposited sand and mud, layer over layer, from the materials that were ejected from the exploding mountains. Lava erupted from fissures into the sea water here to form the oddly shaped deposits found within the sand and mud at these falls.

These falls were dangerous during the logging days. It is said that Peter Lougee was a new and young lumberjack, who just appeared to a logging gang one winter. The gang he chose to work with were working in the Allagash region. No one knew where he came from, or how old he was. He said he was eighteen years old, but he could have been much younger. It really did not matter; the boy was willing to work, so he signed up, and was sent to work in gang number thirteen with twenty-four seasoned men.

During this particular winter, they were going to cut the lumber along a certain tract along the river. The men set up camp for the first few days, seeming to get along together with few arguments. It was during the second week at camp that the jokes started.

One day, grease was put on the grindstone, which hung in a frame close by the camp door. There was a pan of grease in the fire-pit, where the men greased their moccasins. This entire pan of hot grease had been poured over the grindstone, completely encasing it. It was annoying to the men to clean off this important logging tool, and if they ever found out who had done this, there would be payment due.

The next morning, the same joke was played. Perhaps, the men thought, they were cursed. After all, look at the number of their work crew—thirteen. Loggers are very superstitious people, by nature, so being cursed for any number of reasons was not far from their thoughts at any given time. The crew boss decided that he better stay awake to see what was happening, and who was causing this needless work for his men. Of course, nothing happened for two nights. On the third night, the boss saw an outline of a man pouring grease on the grindstone. It was Peter. The boss caught him, cuffed him, and sent him back to his bunk, with a promise of a birch whipping if he was caught again.

The next day, Peter was chastised again, but claimed to know nothing about what happened. He denied everything, including talking to the boss the night before. He claimed that he walked in his sleep, and maybe that was what had happened. However, no one believed him.

A week later, every pipe in camp (every lumberjack smoked a pipe) was saturated with the offensive whale oil that was burned in lamps. This caused a major uproar. This was a serious offense, so the boss decided that this joke needed to be handled by his men. The men took Peter down to the river, cut a hole in the ice, and dunked him, until he could not speak or stand. After this incident, ten days passed without another joke being played.

The next joke that Peter played was to put molasses on the "deacon's seat." The "deacon's seat" was the long bench that sat at the foot of the bunks in all the logging camps. It was where the men sat to eat their meals and to put their boots on. It was also the *only* place to sit in the logging camp, except for the floor or ground. The molasses was poured along the entire length of the bench, and many of the men sat in the syrupy mess in the dark, because the sun had not risen yet. The boss decided that he had better intervene this time, because the men suggested that perhaps they should just break Peter's neck, and be done with him. The boss grilled Peter, but all Peter did was grin and deny doing anything the night before.

There was not much more that the boss could do. He could flog Peter, but he did not believe that it would do any good. He could fire Peter, but Peter was one of the best choppers in the gang. The boss did not want to let Peter go, but something had to be done, because he knew that he might not be able to stop the men from killing Peter, if Peter played another joke.

It was decided that Peter would have to sleep in the "wangin." The term comes from *Wangan* or *ahwangan*, which is an Abenaki word that refers to all the impediments that are associated with canoe travel. An ahwangan is a portage or canoe carried from one navigable stream to the next. It is a metaphor for the laborious process of traveling from one watershed to the next, carrying both the canoe and cargo overland. This particular wangin that Peter was to sleep in was a large chest that carried the axes, peavies, ropes, and other items needed by the loggers. It was seven feet long and four feet wide with a clasp that could only be opened from the outside. There was a hole in it, enough for Peter to breathe.

When Peter was told where he was going to sleep, he had to be forced into the chest. He screamed to be let out, but stopped after the men threw cold water into the chest. From that day on, Peter would be forced into the wangin every night. On March 29th that year, it was finally time to drive the cut logs down river. The wangin was needed to carry the tools, so Peter was allowed to sleep with the crew—until he played another joke. The story does not state what he did, but it is said that it was very bad. From then on, Peter was forced to sleep in the wangin every night. The wangin was emptied every night, but it stayed on the boat, which was moored on shore.

One morning, when the drive was below Round Pond, about seven miles from Allagash Falls, it was discovered that the boat, wangin, and Peter were missing. It was assumed that the boat had not been moored properly, and had down the river with the wangin and Peter still on board.

The gang went to look for the missing boat, wangin, and Peter, and they found the wangin at the bottom of the falls. It was full of water, but Peter was nowhere to be found. The boat was wrecked further down river. Whatever happened that night, Peter was never seen or heard from again. No one ever inquired about him, nor did he ever ask for his wages from working all winter.

Everyone was puzzled by this event. It appeared that Peter died after going over the falls, but no body was ever found. The men in the logging gang believed it was just another of Peter's jokes, that he'd found a way out of the wangin, set the boat off, and left the camp, probably grinning all the way. On the other hand, it is equally possible that Peter died during his ride over the falls, and the river swept his body away.

Perhaps it is his face that is seen in the falls at times.

Unknown Aroostook Settlers

There is one other strange unknown mystery that still exists in the County. When the area became a county in 1839, it was a hearty soul who could put down roots in the unexplored region. Why is it then, that when the first pioneers came to the area near Salmon Brook, near Washburn, they found thirty cabins, obviously built before any permanent settlers came there?

These thirty cabins were actually tumble-down huts, built in groups of five cabins—constructed not near the river, but far in the woods, seemingly out of sight. They were built out of small trees and poles, around six inches in diameter, which proves that the builders used axes and saws to accomplish their tasks. The cabins were small and low, with shed roofs, covered with spruce or pine bark. This also seems to prove that the cabins were built in the summer, when this bark was peeling from the trees. There were no floors in the cabins, but there were cut blocks of wood inside, perhaps used as seats. Fireplaces stood in the centers of the cabins' rooms, with holes cut above for the smoke to escape.

Who built them? A number of theories have arisen—the first being the possibility that some of the Native American St.

Francis members, the ones who refused to go to Canada when forced, built them. Probably not, though. Native Americans did not built huts, and they probably would not have used saws to build.

The second theory is that perhaps the Acadians came to this area while running from the British, and built this small community. Probably not. The Acadians built substantial log cabins with double-steeped roofs, covered with cedar or pine splits.

The third theory is that the cabins were built by trappers who came down from Canada to catch the fur creatures of the area. Probably not. There are too many cabins to be built for trappers. They do not travel in groups of thirty or so. Also, the cabins are too far from the river to be of any use to the fur trapper. Last, trappers do not trap in the summer, when these cabins were obviously built.

The last theory is that perhaps criminals sought shelter in the Maine woods from lawmakers. This is probable. In 1794, a ship set sail from England. Its destination was the penal colony at Van Diemen Land on Australia's southern coast. The ship held one hundred and ninety convicts. As the ship rounded the Cape of Good Hope, and was just entering the Indian Ocean, a storm struck. The ship was on the verge of sinking, so the crew fearing immediate death, let some of the convicts free to help them keep the ship afloat.

The convicts seemed to turn the tide and the ship was saved. The convicts decided that they were not going to return to the hold, and after a long, bloody battle, and though both sides lost many men, the convicts eventually won. The remaining crew were tossed overboard.

Alexander McVane was the leader of the convict revolt and a pretty good sailor. He was chosen by his convict crew as the Captain. He knew the only way to be free was to sail to the great forests of Canada to escape. The crew agreed, and they headed as fast as they could to the Gulf of the St. Lawrence River.

Three months later, in May 1794, the citizens of Quebec, Canada, awoke to the cries of a fire near the waters edge. A sailing vessel had apparently run aground in the night and was on fire. The people ran to help the sailors, but no one was aboard. The vessel was completely destroyed, but no bodies were ever found. On the path leading out of town, there were the footprints of many men, and sensing something was not right, soldiers were sent to search for the missing crew.

Later that night, the soldiers were surrounded by a hundred rough looking men, all carrying pistols and cutlasses. These men ordered the soldiers to turn around or die. The rough looking men took their muskets, ammunition, food and supplies, then disappeared into the darkness. The soldiers returned to Quebec with their story.

A new group of soldiers followed the men to the border of Maine, where the men seemed to have disappeared. They were never heard from again.

The mystery cabin builders did not seem to have died near their cabins. There are no tools or graves found in the area. The cabins just appear to have been deserted.

One last point to mention here is that the Native Americans that lived near the Aroostook River told a story that in the years before any European was seen in the area, strange looking men, calling themselves Swiss sailors, came to the area and settled. They took Micmac wives and lived in the area until they died natural deaths. The mystery of the cabins still is not explained today.

The First New England Settlers

Now, back to the story of the people who existed in northern New England in the earliest eras. There was an ancient group of people who lived in northern New England, but who disappeared without a trace. Not even the modern Native American tribes, who lived in New England when the Europeans first arrived, know exactly who these people were or what happened to them.

Scientists can deduce some things about these people from what little has been found. They made flint spears points and arrowheads, as well as skinning knives. They also used weighted rawhide, which was thrown to entangle the legs of game to bring it down for the kill. These weapons were also decorated with little three-petal flowers, which show the love of nature that these people may have had. They used the spear for hunting; the bow and arrow was not yet invented.

No clothes or shelters exist from this time. They probably wore skins and furs, and lived in shelters made from the brush. They seem to have had the ability to make fire, but they may have eaten their food raw. The climate in Maine was much warmer and drier during the time that they lived there, so they did not get the cold that is experienced today. During this time, this state was like an island, there was so much water surrounding it. As the ice from the glacier melted, the water started to drain south, thus creating the rivers and lakes that are enjoyed today.

They may have been the first people to use roads in New England. It is believed that they may have used the "horsebacks" found all around the region. These are glacial gravel deposits that are also known as kames or eskers. They are firm and well drained areas, but they are also crooked and can be compared to walking on a roller coaster.

The one thing that we do know about these people is that they buried their members in graves filled with hematite, which is iron ore called red ochre. They buried their dead in Maine, sometime between 2500 BC and 1800 BC. Actually, these graves are the only places that we have found regarding these people. The cemeteries seem to be on the coast, but not even the Native Americans who lived here have stories about the existence of these people.

The Native American village that still exists on Indian Island in the Penobscot River is called *ne-gan-o-den-ek*, which means "old town," but there are still no legends to describe the ways of the Red Paint people as they have been called. The first settlers were terrified when they found these graves filled with red clay. They thought that the graves were the work of the "devil" and in some cases, the family would move off the property, believing that it must be haunted.

The fact that that are so many graves in so many different areas of the Maine coast, it can be surmised that the people were numerous, or they lived here a very long time. Unfortunately, not many bones have been found, but what little has been recovered, has been identified as human. Though the bones did not last the test of time, the red paint did. It still looks fresh and will stick to the hand when touched. It also does not come off easily, so perhaps it is no wonder that the early settlers were unnerved when they found the graves. All Red Paint cemeteries are near water that was navigable by a small boat, however, there is usually little surface indication of their presence.

It can also be surmised that death had rituals attached to it for these people. The cemeteries show planning and perhaps some sort of a belief in life after death. The people must have had some sense of a culture. One strange item found in many of the graves were the items needed for making a fire. Apparently, it was thought that the dead would need to be able to make a fire, wherever they were going after they died.

There are usually several quarts of red ochre found in the graves, but nothing more about why this substance was put in the graves can be deduced. Perhaps it was believed that the red clay would preserve the body in some way. Perhaps it reminded the people of blood. No one knows for sure.

There was definitely some magical aspect attached to the clay to be buried with the dead. The burial practices show a well developed ceremonial life, somehow dealing with the red ochre. It seems unlikely that the clay was just used for a decoration. It is a long trip over difficult terrain to get the clay. The only source of this red clay is from a pit on the side of Mount Katahdin, the highest spot in Maine. Some of the graves are quite a distance from this spot, so the red clay must have been important to obtain and then place into the grave.

Another strange item that was found in the graves were spear points made of translucent quartzite, but where this material came from in Maine is unknown today. Necklaces were also found, made with little blue stones that were carved into slender crescents and pierced—so they could be put on a throng perhaps?

Tools have also been found in the cemeteries. It seems that the Red Paint People were unequaled and very advanced in the stone age they lived in. The quality of the tools show that these people took great pride in their work, creating long, slender spears, daggers, plummets, gouges, square-edged hatchets, and adze blades. They fashioned a hexagonal spear point that was not made in any other primitive race in North America at the time. There have also been beaver tooth chisels, as well as hammer stones found in the graves. Many of these tools have been authenticated by the Smithsonian Museum in Washington, D. C.

Because their dead were found near water, it appears that these people lived near the water and used dugouts as boats. The canoe had not been invented here yet. It was much faster when one could travel on water in this locale, than on horseback roads or through the immense, vast forests!

One strange treasure that may have been left by the Red Paint people on the water's edge is the five million cubic feet of oyster shells that have been discovered on both sides of the Damariscotta River. There is a sharp bend westward in this river on its journey to Damariscotta Lake, and at this bend, these ancient and mysterious shell heaps or shell middens have been found.

At one time, these mounds were seemingly unending and gigantic. Over the past fifty years, however, they have been removed to make lime; for walk ways, roads, and other purposes. The huge heaps can now only be seen in old photos and in the memory of people who were lucky enough to actually see them. It is thought that not all the mounds have been excavated and that some still exist on the banks of the river. These heaps are considered so ancient, that it has been estimated that half of the deposits have just wasted away through the eon of time.

What is remarkable about this area is that there are no villages, no kitchens, no relics, or anything else that may explain what the people were doing there. Some theories are that this may have been a garbage site, not a place to eat or live. The size of the oyster shell amazes scholars today. The smallest shell found was a foot in length and nearly twenty inches long! Oysters do not live in the river today, but they are indigenous to the coast of Maine. However, as the coast of Maine grew colder, the environmental conditions that favor oysters there declined. It is known today that oysters no longer live farther north than Cape Cod, Massachusetts. It is just too cold.

There is a theory as to what may have happened to the villages and sites of these remarkable people. Maine was once much higher above the sea than it now. Some of the mountain tops of yesterday are islands today. The glacier that covered Maine was 10,000 feet thick and dropped the sea level over 300 feet. The beach zone was almost one hundred miles farther out to sea than it is today. The glacier melt caused the sea to rise and created the submerged coastline. The sea moved inland almost seventy-five miles.

It is interesting to note that this process would be very slow. The Red Paint People would be living on a slowly sinking land mass, and would be able to move inland before being overwhelmed by water. Perhaps they moved their most sacred items, for example, their graves, to the higher place to preserve them, or perhaps they always buried their dead far away from their lives.

It should also be noted here that there is a major earth-quake fault, called the Fundian fault-scarp, that lies on the northwest side of the Bay of Fundy near Casco Bay. Perhaps it was an earthquake that sank the land where the Red Paint People once lived and only their cemeteries that existed on higher ground remained. It may be that the answer to some of the Red Paint People questions lie on the ocean bottom.

There are other theories that the Red Paint People were really non-Native Americans from the mythical town of Norumbega, though, as proven in earlier chapters, that village never existed. Another theory is that the Red Paint People were wiped out by tidal wave from the Atlantic Ocean. It has also been thought that an ocean-slide, ocean-quake, volcanic explosion, or hurricane may have been responsible for the disappearance of these people. It is not believed that the Red Paint People merged with any other people or Native Ameri-can tribes that eventually settled in the area, nor does it look like they migrated to another place. The Red Paint People may have died catastrophically, with no one left to tell others who came to the land after them. It would then seem that this ancient and civilized people disappeared into thin air.

Haunted Brooksville

There is one other place that has a legend about an old Native American village and of a battle that took place there, but exactly who lived here remains a mystery. This Native American village was supposedly in Brooksville, and the battle that took place on the southern end of Walker's Pond, which was also known as Gray's Pond. The year was around 1600, so the legend goes. The Native Americans would send raiding parties to plunder the ships that would sail into Eggemoggin Reach. In the Spring of this year, they killed the crew of a fishing vessel and burned the ship.

The Europeans sent out an expedition to find the culprits, and they are said to have found someone from the raiding party. By sparing his life, he led them to the village. No one in the village survived the retaliation.

The real question is, did this village really exist? Arrow heads, spear points, and human bones have been found in the area. To make this place even more enchanted and haunted, there are two wild plants that are purportedly only found on the site of this supposed Native American village, and no where else in Maine. There is a large variety of yellow violet and a species of liquorice with roots that are very sweet. Why these plants grow here, no one knows. Were they planted there by the Native Americans who once lived there? Did these plants just grow there naturally, and did the Native Americans just come there to pick the plants? Again, no one really knows.

There is another reason that this area may be considered haunted. The first industry in the newly incorporated town was a saw mill. There were several saw mills in the town, but the one with the unsolved mystery attached is the saw mill at Goose Falls. The story goes that the one-time and only owner of the Goose Falls saw mill had to borrow quite a bit of money to finance his venture. As sometimes happens with a new struggling business, this owner was not making very much money and consequently apparently was not able to pay his bills when they were due.

One day, a stranger came to town and asked for directions to the saw mill. Directions were given to the person, and the stranger was seen heading toward the mill. That was the last time that anyone ever saw the stranger. No one saw him leave the mill area or town. There was not even a body to be found. It appeared that he just disappeared into thin air. Shortly after this happened, the mill owner just closed up the mill and walked away, never to return. No one knew where he was going, and the mill remained idle and abandoned for so long that the mill owner's name has been forgotten over the time span.

It was after a long while that the residents of town noticed that bright lights would often be seen in the old mill buildings and around the area at night, when no one was supposed to be around. The light was often seen between the hours of midnight and early morning near the old water wheel. After the light would disappear, the old water wheel would start to spin, very slowly at first, and then move faster and faster, until it was going at full force.

This raised great curiosity around town, and many residents claimed that they went up to the old mill to investigate when the old water wheel would start to spin. When they would peek into the windows, they claimed to see a headless man riding a log, head first, or where his head was suppose to be, directly into the teeth of the old, now rusty, saw.

A theory quickly arose as to what the cause of this apparition could be. It was believed that the stranger had been a bill collector, who came to collect the money that was owed by the mill owner. The mill owner either got angry or scared because he could not pay his bills, so he threw the stranger into the saw, either by accident or on purpose, and the stranger was be-headed. This is not a proven fact, rather it is just speculation. Perhaps the truth will never be known.

Great Chebeague Island

So, while the prehistoric people who lived in northern New England remains a mystery, what *is* known is that the retreating glacier created the many islands that were discovered by the first explorers to the coast line. Great Chebeague Island was the island where the first European settlers, as early as the eighteenth century, found life-sized stone carvings in an ancient Celtic style under layers of sea moss. Who left them and why they were there is still under investigation. There is also a legend about this particular island saying that Captain Kidd buried treasure there. Whatever happened there, it is considered an enchanted place.

Isles of Shoals

There is a group of islands off the New England coast, some which belong to Maine and the rest belong to New Hampshire, called the Isles of Shoals, which have many alleged buried treasures and ghosts to guard them.

"It is quite impossible to give an idea of these rocky shores, how confusedly they are bound together, lying in all direction: what solid ledges, what great fragments thrown out from the rest...as if some of the massive materials of the world remained superfluous after the Creator had finished, and were carelessly thrown down here, where the millionth part of them emerged from the sea, and in the course of thousands of years have become partially bestrewn with a little soil. Pour the blue sea around these islets, and let the surf whitten and steal up from their points, the northwest wind the while raising thousands of whitecaps..."

—America's First Novelist, Nathaniel Hawthorne, after he first
visited the Isles of Shoals.

The Isles of Shoals are a group of nine islands that was discovered by the Spanish, when they landed on them in 1635. Geologists say that they were once the high spots of hilly regions, which were depressed during the glacial period. Though they regained some of their mass, the coast never regained all of it, and have become the islands that we know today.

The Maine islands are Duck Island, Appledore or Hog Island, Malaga Island, Smuttynose Island, and Cedar Island. The New Hampshire islands are: Star Island, Lunging or Londoner Island, White Isand, and Seavey Island. Actually, the number of islands changes with the tides. At high tide, there are only eight islands, White and Seavey become one island. At low tide, there are nine islands, as White and Seavey separate, and as hard as it is to believe, grass does grow on this narrow strip of land that is often under the sea.

The Isles of Shoals are located six miles from the mouth of the Piscataqua River and are very desolate, barren, and forbidding. Their shores would daunt anyone from approaching them for fear of being shipwrecked. The name, however, does not come from the ragged reefs near the area, but from the shoaling, or schooling, of large numbers of fish. There are very few trees on the islands and little vegetation. Until 1647, no women were allowed on the islands, but over four hundred men lived and fished there.

In 1616, John Smith called these islands Smith or Smythe Isles after himself. The name did not stay with the area. Most of the islands at that time were overgrown with shrubs because there were no trees. The wind blasted the islands in the winter and the trees did not survive.

There were many wrecks on these shores, especially before the age of lighthouses. There were many deaths, and at times, the sea would wash cargo on the shores of the islands. Usually the ship would completely break up and the cargo would be strewn for miles all along the ocean floor.

Why was this desolate area ever settled? The answer again is simple economics. This area was considered a superior fishing spot. There was a new type of fish created here called "dunfish" or "dumbfish." Dunning meant that a fish taken on shore was ripped open, had its' head cut off and removed viscera. The fishermen would then cut out the backbone and the two halves were salted and piled in bulk to cure for ten to twenty hours. The fish were washed and laid out on flakes and frames to dry in the sun and "sweat" in the storehouse, until ready for market. They were then cut into transparent strips the color of brown sherry wine. This fish was so superior, that the price of fish worldwide was quoted from these islands at one time. Just to make matters more dangerous, there were also four-foot sand sharks that swam in the waters near these islands.

The island residents were not pirates, but some were smugglers or wreck salvagers, and when pirates frequently visited the islands, the islanders were more or less friendly with them. In 1686, there was an order that went out from the Massachusetts Council—remember that the state of Maine was still a part of Massachusetts until 1820 when it became a state as part of the Missouri Compromise—that ships could not deliver any part of the lading they carried at the Isles of Shoals, without first contacting the Customs Officer of the area. The authorities believed there was too much smuggling going on there, and the records of the era show that this was a favorite spot for smugglers and pirates, hence the numerous legends of buried treasure and ghosts.

There are four legends that are not connected to a particular island in the Isles of Shoals, but are connected to the entire region. The first legend tells us that no Native American canoe would ever go to these islands. The people living in the area before the Europeans came considered it a "bad" place. It was considered bad luck or one would become cursed, if one ever visited the islands.

The second legend is that a ghost of a monk walks on the Isles and his presence tells of a coming gale. He walks along the island shore, and glances out at the heaving seas, but the wind and rain do not seem to bother him, not even ruffling his hair or clothes.

The third legend tells of treasure buried on the Isles by a Captain Larramore, or Larrimore, of the *Larramore Galley*. Larramore turned pirate and just before he was captured, it is said that a small boat with some of his crew on it was seen heading either toward or away from the Isles of Shoals back to the main ship. When the vessel was finally boarded, only forty-two ounces of gold was found. It is believed that the ship carried much more loot, and that it was buried on one of the islands in the Isles of Shoals.

The last legend is that, after the murder of a woman on one of the islands by a crewman from a Guinea boat in the early 1900s, the murderer escaped to Boston. The woman's husband was accused of the murder, but escaped in a Dory and was never seen again. Supposedly, he drowned out in the sea. Since that time, the crews of all Guinea boats were attacked and wrecked for the next twenty years near these islands in the middle of a storm or on foggy nights. Eventually, the boats stopped coming to the area—and who could blame them? What did those crews encounter in the ocean? Perhaps, it was some*one*, not some*thing*. There were never any survivors, so no one really knows.

Duck Island

This island got its name because it had a swampy freshwater pond in its center where wild ducks in migration paused for a rest.

It is also possible that the pirate Ned Low buried an undisclosed amount of treasure here.

Londoner's or Lunging Island

This island was either named for a ship that was wrecked there, or for the London company that sent a fleet consisting of four ships there, in 1615, to establish a trading post. This was the island where seamen came to careen their vessels, which means to clean and paint the hulls of their ships. The pirate Blackbeard is also supposedly to have set up a base of operations on this island. This treasure is said to be buried at the landing side of the beach facing the Star Island Hotel, halfway across the half moon stretch of the beach. There is more on Blackbeard and these islands later in this chapter.

Cedar Island

This island was named for the old cedar grove that was found here in 1614. There were the only trees visible on the islands at this time and only three or four trees remained the year that it was discovered.

Malaga Island

This island was named because it reminded the Spanish who landed here of the vineyards back home.

White Island

This is the southern island of the Isles of Shoals, and it is only two acres of barren land. It was named for an ancestor of Captain Joseph White, who was born on Hog or Appledore Island in 1750 and murdered in Salem, Massachusetts, on April 6, 1830. The western part of this island is sometimes Seavey Island, when the tide is low. No one knows where that name originated. This island is created of pale gneiss rock. The other major question about this island is about where the land actually comes from. No one really knows. The rock seems to have simply risen up from the bottom of the sea for no known reason. The adjacent waters are sparkling bright. This fact alone makes the island very mysterious.

Legends state that there are numerous treasures to be found on this island. It is important to remember that island life is very different then life on the mainland. The sea surrounding the island can lead to a good life, or a not so good life.

Storms lash the coast and island with a violence that is not always understood on the mainland. They are blasted with high winds and very high waves. Treasure that may have been buried there could be pushed deeper into the sand or swept completely away into the ocean. It is even possible that treasure from the ocean is pushed onto the shore, making it a good idea to check the beach after a storm. The islands are also victim to the seiche, which is a stationary wave movement. This causes very unusual tides on nearby beaches. For every one-inch drop in barometric pressure, there is a thirteen-inch increase in the ocean. During the gale of November 29, 1945, the seas swept away three small outhouses near the lighthouse, ripped the planking off the bell tower, and exposed an old building foundation. No one even knew that building existed. The waves went completely over the top of the ninety-foot lighthouse tower. At the height of the storm, the waves crashed through kitchen doors, up to the waists of the lighthouse residents.

All that said, what better place to hide a treasure, then on a place where nature can be cruel and not many visitors will want to visit? There are three pirates who may have chosen this island to bury their treasure and then murdered someone to protect it.

In 1714, the notorious pirate, Blackbeard, is said to have had a crewmember, or even his first officer, called Scot. Other versions of the story say that it was the pirate Sandy Gordon, and not Blackbeard who had a crewman called Scot. Names are often changed in history, mainly due to poor writing and spelling errors. Also, many people were illiterate. To keep matters simple, the name for this story will stay Scot, who is part of Blackbeard's crew. The legend tells that Scot was a crewmember of a pirate ship called the *Porpoise*. The Captain, for some unsaid reason, decided to bring his beautiful daughter, Martha, on board for a trip, and Scot decided that he wanted her. He went to her cabin, had his way with her, and was caught. The Captain lashed him seventy-two times for his tryst with his daughter.

Scot decided that it was time he was Captain of this ship, so he inspired a mutiny to occur. (Remember, according to the pirate law, the Captain is not allowed to give punishment to the crew.) Scot is said to have lashed the Captain to death, and took Martha as his wife or mistress, no one is really sure.

Eventually, this pirate was so good at his craft that he caught the attention of the infamous Blackbeard. It is said that Blackbeard asked him to be part of his crew. If you believe the other version, it is said that the pirate Gordon and Blackbeard started to work together, and Blackbeard was impressed with Scot during that time. Due to the nature of pirates, that piece of the story does not fit. However it happened, Scot eventually became a part of Blackbeard's crew.

Blackbeard is said to taken plunder from a Spanish ship near the Isles of Shoals, and that Scot and his wife buried his part of the loot on this island. Scot returned to Blackbeard's ship, leaving his wife, who was said to be alive, to guard the treasure. Scot supposedly died in a battle and never returned to White Island. The blonde woman supposedly died on the island, and her ghost still guards the treasure buried at the low point of the island, while waiting for her lover to return.

Appledore Island in Maine also claims this story. It is said that Scot married Martha Herring of Appledore Island. Scot is said to have whipped Martha's father to death, with Martha a willing participant. Martha, however, is said to be dressed in red, not white, when she is seen staring out at the sea awaiting her lover's return.

Sandy Gordon, an eighteenth century pirate, who was said to be a first mate or pirate partner to Blackbeard, is also said to have buried his entire wealth on this island. Gordon was said to be ruthless, evil, and insane. He sounds a lot like Blackbeard in this way. He was said to have been a captain of the pirate ship, *Porpoise*, but his crew mutinied, so he signed on with Blackbeard. He was so successful with Blackbeard that he eventually got another ship, *The Flying Scot*, and supposedly acquired millions of dollars of wealth, when he came to White Island. He built a cabin and buried all his loot near it. The treasure is said to consist of gold and silver coins and jewels.

Gordon still thought that it was a good idea to pirate the area and did not want to retire to a quiet island life. Within a year of burying all his loot there, his ship was involved in a battle with an English Man-Of-War. Gordon realized that he was not going to win this battle, and he knew that he was going to be hanged if caught, so he blew up his ship. He never returned for his loot on White Island.

It is obvious that something happened there, on one of the islands, and that pirate treasure can still be found.

What is difficult when hunting for treasure is that the names are all the same, but mixed up in some way. *The Flying Scot*, the crewman Scot, Blackbeard or Gordon, Appledore or White Island...Is it possible that the story gets confusing on purpose, so the treasure remains hidden?

To add more treasure to the story, the pirate, Quelch, is said to have buried $100,000 on this island in 1702. Though the Massachusetts Militia apparently caught Quelch burying gold and silver on the Isles, they could not find it.

In 1867, a fisherman is said to have dug up one hundred pounds of gold bullion and an undisclosed amount of coins. There is treasure on this island and some of it has been found. It is interesting to note here, however, that there is not much dirt on this rocky island to bury as much treasure here as has been reported. It is said that the grass that does grow on the land between White and Seavey Islands is just enough for the lighthouse keepers cow to graze on.

Smuttynose Island

This long and narrow island was named because of a smutch of dark seaweed on the nose of the rock that extends into the sea from the southeast corner. The first treasure legend of this island is that the pirate, Blackbeard, supposedly buried an immense treasure of gold ingots here. The treasure is said to be just below the waterline on the beach east of the breakwater.

Historians agree that Blackbeard did take a bride to Smuttynose Island for a honeymoon—exactly what number bride she was, no one knows. She was also left here to guard the treasure that he buried there around 1720. Blackbeard did leave the area, when a large British fleet appeared over the horizon, and never returned for his bride or his loot. She died there in 1735. Her ghost, blonde with blue eyes, supposedly appears and looks to the sea, saying over and over again, "He will come again." She never seems to pay attention to anyone who sees her, and she never appears anywhere else or does anything different. This story sounds a lot like Scot's wife on

White Island, or perhaps this story took place on Appledore Island. This is the reason that seeking treasure can be very confusing at times.

Treasure has been found on this island, though. Sometime before 1820, Captain Samuel Haley, a resident of the shipping village on the island called Gosport, uncovered four silver bars on shore that were worth $4,000. The treasure was found just below the waterline on the beach, east of the breakwater at Smuttynose.

Does this story sound familiar? It is the same tale that was told about Blackbeard in the prior paragraph. The story also is told another way. Haley was building a seawall, turned over a large flat stone, and beneath the stone, lay bars of solid silver. He used the money to connect a seawall from Smuttynose to Malaga Island to make a safe harbor for all ships. Haley built a tavern and windmill on the island with timber that washed on shore from ship wrecks. He was also the island's first lighthouse keeper. He kept a lantern burning every night in the east window of his home before the lighthouse was built in 1820. The light overlooked the open sea and Cedar Island Ledge. This area is noted for the many shipwrecks that took place along these shores.

There is another reason why Haley may have found that silver. On January 14, 1813, a rich Spanish ship, the name given is *Sagunto* (but that is not true), was wrecked on the island. A silver watch was found that had stopped at 4:00, with the initials P. S. on the back. Many men were washed on shore and Haley was living on the island at the time. It is said that fourteen men from this wreck were buried on the island.

However, ground penetrating radar over the supposed graves of people who are buried on the island showed no human remains. To this day, Spanish pieces of eight do wash up on shore from time to time, perhaps from this wreck.

There are four other pirates who also may have buried treasure here. Quelch, Ned Low, and William Fly, who was a bloodthirsty pirate, but only lasted as a pirate for thirty-five days before he was caught and hanged in Boston. The fourth pirate was Captain Rachel Wall, the last female pirate in New England. She stole a Gloucester schooner and headed to Smuttynose, taking over a house that already existed on the island as a base of operations. She was successful at plundering ships in the area by using a never before used tactic of piracy. Her schooner would lie in wait in the lee of Star Island, and after a major storm, Wall would go out into the sea, put up a distress flag, making it appear that she was the only female survivor of a shipwreck. A rescue was usually attempted, and then Wall would attack. Eventually, she was caught and hanged at twenty-nine years of age on October 8, 1789. It is not unreasonable to believe that she may have buried some of her loot on Smuttynose.

Star Island

This island was named for the broken crags that extend in all directions from the island, like the spangles of a star. There is an old superstition on this island that a person walking along the beach would find or see a spade sticking out of the ground. The person usually notes the spot, but is not ready to dig right then for whatever reason. The person returns to the spot later, and the spade is gone. The person will then spend his life wondering what may have been hidden there. William Mace, a long ago resident, swore that he had that experience.

Another version of this old tale is that another person saw the spade, passed by, then turned back to see it sinking into the ground, along with a golden flat iron. The person grabbed onto the gold, but could not keep it from returning to the ground.

It is said that a fisherman was paddling in his Dory, which is the Yankee version or descendant of a Viking ship, just around the southeast point to explore the caves and to look for driftwood on the island. At this time, the island was uninhabited, and he saw glittering coins in the shallow water. Apparently, he believed that this was the remains of some long lost shipwreck. He quickly filled his pockets with all the coins he could find.

There is another story about the caves on this island that occurred in the 1700s. Star Island had a fort built to protect the residents from Native American raids. Apparently, the Native Americans got over their fear of going over to these islands when the Europeans came. Betty Moody Cave is the location where Betty Moody, an island resident, and her children, hid during a Native American attack. It is said that she had to smother her small children to keep them quiet, so they would not be found. The mother and child are said to still haunt the area. Sounds of adult and child crying are said to still be heard near this cave.

A three-legged black pot filled with gold and silver pieces was found on this island in the late 1800s.

The pirate, John Quelch, supposedly buried $275,000 on this island. Only half of it was ever found. Quelch buried one hundred weight of gold dust, thousands of gold and silver coins, silks and taffeta from the *Whydah* somewhere. A 1950 *Life* Magazine article states that it is possible that $100,000 worth of treasure may still be buried on this island.

During World War II, government representatives supposedly visited the island and found evidence of substantial amounts of silver on the landing side of the beach, facing the Star Island Hotel. The exact location is half way across the half moon stretch of the beach. The silver bars were so far down that it would be too expensive to get them out. So, the government decided against this venture. Allegedly, in 1950, a photo from a plane with film sensitive to gold and silver showed evidence of those elements on the island, but no treasure has ever been claimed.

Appledore or Hog Island

This island is three hundred acres of bay and huckleberry bushes, wild roses and lots of vegetation, at least compared to the rest of the islands in this group. It is the largest of the group and its first name was Hog Island, supposedly because it resembled a corpulent hog, wallowing in brine. The name of Appledore Island comes from an English fishing village on Barnstable Bay. In 1826, the island was uninhabited because in the 1680s, the state of Maine had assessed taxes for the island inhabitants. The forty families who lived on the island decided that they would rather live in New Hampshire than pay Maine taxes, so they dismantled their homes and moved to Star Island in New Hampshire.

There is a legend about this island that tells of some young people, who were camping on the south side of the island, digging up a skeleton. The skull had three indentations, as if made by a sharp instrument, like a Native American tomahawk or a pirate cutlass. Whatever killed this person, foul play was definitely suggested.

There are stories of a Spanish wreck here too. The cargo was broad silver pieces that were found on the shore. No one knows what the name of this ship was. Perhaps it may be that the silver pieces came from a ship wreck out to sea.

The pirate, Quelch, is said to have buried nine pounds of gold and one hundred and ninety pounds of silver or two hundred bars of silver on the west side of the island. It is also said that Blackbeard buried a treasure on the side of the island that faces the Star Island Hotel across the water. The story about Scot's lover protecting his buried treasure is also said to have taken place on this island, not on White Island.

The legend of this island and the Blackbeard treasure's ghostly guard is that she wears a dark cape that covers her blonde hair, and her face is beautiful, wan, and she also has blue eyes. By those who have witnessed this ghost walking along the shore looking out to sea, it is said that the wild wind never ruffles her clothes or hair, and her feet never crunch on the shells or sand she is walking on. It is said that a treasure is really buried on this island, however, it is not Blackbeard's treasure, which may be buried on Londoner's Island, but it is Scot's treasure, and he left his lover to guard it with her life and beyond. That is what she is still doing to this day.

It is important to note here that the search for buried treasure must be done with patience and with a grain of salt.

It must be remembered that people did not want the seeker to find the buried treasure. Misnaming the place where it was buried or using vague landmarks was only one way to mislead the treasure hunter.

There is a story about the native shoaler, Philip Babb, who lived on the island. He was supposedly one of Captain Kidd's men, who is seen as a ghost with a ring around a scrawny neck, as if his throat was cut or he was hanged. The ghost dresses in a coarse striped butchers' frock with a leather belt, containing a knife, which was always sharp and glittering. He is considered a horrifying and fearsome specter with a villainous and pale face, and snaky, greasy hair and whiskers.

"Old Bab," as the ghost is called, lived in the valley between the north and south hills of the island. The valley ends on the east side in Broad Cove and on the west side in Babb's Cove. His house was on the south hillside, near the cove that bears his name. He ran a tavern and a butcher's shop on the island. He died in 1671. At the head of Babb's Cove, Babb's supposedly buried some of Kidd's loot. The pit was said to be thirty feet across and ten feet deep. He supposedly buried an iron chest, but it is said to be too heavy to get out of the pit. This is the treasure that his ghost guards.

After the coast guard built a boathouse over that spot, his ghost has disappeared. The only problem in believing that this legend may be true, is that Babbs died in 1671, and Kidd became a privateer in 1696. If something is buried by Babbs on this island, it was not part of Kidd's loot, nor was he ever a member of Kidd's crew. One of the shoals just off this island is called Babb's Rock for Philip Babbs.

An interesting side note to this story is that it is also said that the ghost that guards the pirate treasure is really the pirate, John Quelch himself. He is guarding his own treasure that he supposedly buried on this island.

These shoals are still dangerous, even in the twentieth century. On July 17, 1902, fourteen employees from the Oceanic Hotel located on the island were taking a cruise around the island, when a sudden squall came up and wrecked the boat. All were drowned within 200 feet of the Hotel.

So, it appears that some treasure has been found on these islands, but it would also seem that the ghosts are guarding many more secrets, if one dared to try to find the missing island loot.

Chapter Ten
Casco Bay Islands: Treasure and Ghost Stories of New England's Coast

When the Casco Bay islands off the coast of Maine were first discovered, the explorers thought there were too many to count. They were called the Calendar Islands, because it was thought that there were at least three hundred and sixty-five islands. (The number is actually closer to two hundred and twenty-two islands.) There are also many stories of treasure to be found here. Geologists state that the reason for so many islands in this Bay is because Casco Bay was once the mouth of the Androscoggin River. Eventually, after the building up of debris that completely blocked the mouth, the river had to divert to its present channel, which joins the Kennebec River at Merrymeeting Bay.

Casco Bay is named for two reasons. The first reason is that it is a corruption of the Native American name for this area, *Aucosisco* or "'place of Blue Herons." The second reason is that the Spanish called it *Bahia de Casco* or Casco Bay. There are oral Native American legends of buried treasure in Casco Bay on the Fox Island group, Deer Isle, Vinalhaven, North Haven, Fort Popham, Reef and Ram Islands, Mount Desert Island on Ship Bottom Bay, Monhegan Island, Elm Island, Bailey Island, and Isle Au Haut in Money Cove. These islands were called *Hahkik'watpuk* by the Passamodquoddy tribe. It is said to mean the "great hooded seal place." These animals were common in the area at one time, but have since been exterminated.

Monhegan Island

One of the first islands that the Europeans discovered was Monhegan Island. There have been supposedly Viking marks found on the ledge of the adjacent islet called *Manana*. The marks may have been made in the year 1000 AD. The island was used by the Native Americans of the area as a place for fishing. The fish caught here were incredible, and the main reason why the Europeans settled the region.

The first description of the island was in 1569, as a "great island that was backed like a whale." That was the description of David Ingram, the same man who is said to have started the Norumbega legend. Captain Martin Pring is said to have dropped anchor here in 1603. In 1605, Samuel de Champlain sailed by and called the island "La Nef," because from the sea, the island looked like a ship—at least to him. The island was well known by 1611, and it was the general headquarters for explorers and for fishermen. Captain John Smith came to the island in 1614 to 1616. He is the same person who traveled with Pocahontas, and had seven ships built on this island. Smith was there to mine gold or copper, and described the island as "a high round Isle."

The place where treasure is buried on this island is called *Deadman's Cove*. Legend states that there is a large flat rock over a dead man and treasure chest. The chest just keeps sinking as fast as the treasure seeker can dig. There are also strange moans and thuds heard in the area.

In *Maine Monthly Magazine* in July 1836, this story was told. A patriarch on the island called Trefethren related this story to the reporter about an enchanted treasure that was supposedly found. Many years earlier, two strangers came to the island. They were said to be from Vermont, and came across some family papers that said there was a remarkable rock on a sandy beach on this island. It was a lone rock, and at a given distance from this rock, money could be found by anyone who would dig—observing the spells and incantations needed, of course.

They had found the rock, measured the distance, and now all they had to do was dig. A spirit also guarded the money or gold. The treasure seekers had to dig at midnight, but got nervous, and started to drink brandy to bolster their confidence. They hit a hard substance, and at that moment, the earth shook and one of them fell into the pit. The other ran for help. The rescuers found the man at the bottom of the pit face down. He was unconscious. After the rescuers left, the men continued to dig. After a few days, they left the island, never to be heard from again. All that was found was an empty jar and pot near the pit.

Long Island

Long Island in Casco Bay has an interesting natural phenomena. The beach on the ocean side is called a singing beach, because if the wind and tide are exactly right, a curious musical tone arises from it. The Native Americans also had large shell heaps on this island. It seems that the Native Americans still had feasts on this spot, so the beach singing did not seem to bother them too much.

The singing beach is called Andrews Beach. It does make odd noises at times when the wind blows strongly off the coast. The beach emits a mournful note in a minor key. The phenomenon is attributed to the action of loose particles of sand and small pebbles being swept with great velocity over harder surfaces near the water. It is most notable at low tide.

The real question of this island is: Why does a particular path of white moss, near the spot where the oldest house once stood, turns blood red one day each year? There is a cellar still there on the crest of the hill that is said to be haunted by sounds of clanking heavy chains, sighs, and groans. There was so much noise that no family could occupy the place for any length of time. The house was taken down piece-by-piece and supposedly set up elsewhere with no sounds.

In January 1891, the schooner, *Ada Barker*, was driven on shore on the ledge called *Junk of Pork*. It was quite sometime before any rescue attempt was able to reach the stranded crew, because the storm was so wild, and caused huge waves and strong winds.

When the rescue party finally reached the crew, the rescuers found that they had managed to salvage the cabin doors and canvas from the wreck, and had built a snug shelter. They had hams, beef, a barrel full of flour, and were making fritters and gingerbread dough. They even had frying pans and made fire with the wood from the wreck. The crew managed to survive quite well here.

Coins from shipwrecks are found on the beaches of this island. A ghostly sea captain protects the Long Island treasure. He is seen wrapped in a full-skirted coat, but one can still see the trees through his transparent form.

John's Island

In the eighteenth century, the tavern on the north end of John's Island was a well-known hangout for pirates. It is said that the colonial-style building has $50,000 still buried underneath it. There were rumors of Dutch pirates who visited this island in the early days even before the Europeans arrived. This island is so close to the harbor and fort that it is called a breakwater island or public island. Apparently, the pirates took that to mean that they could use it whenever they needed to.

There was also supposedly a Portuguese pirate who always had plenty of gold and silver to spend, but did not seem to get it from anywhere. He would just show up and there would be plenty to go around. He died in some foreign land and he gave a shipmate a map of this island with a location of a hidden well. He told him that on the bottom of that well, there would be more gold and silver than a half dozen men could carry. He had buried it there himself. When the shipmate returned to John's Island, he found the well, and supposedly one night, he was just about to get the loot out of the well, when a black stallion, eyes blazing, hoofs flying, and nostrils red and flaring, came flying out of the woods. The shipmate dropped everything right there and ran away to safety. He went back three nights in a row, and each night the black stallion would return. Finally, the man gave up, and so the treasure is said to still be in the well. This is apparently a case where the ghost that is guarding the treasure is a favorite animal, who is loyal only to his master.

Jewell Island

Jewell Island has a rich history of buried treasure and ghosts. As alluring as the name is, it probably was named for a fisherman, George Jewell, who purchased it from the Native Americans in 1637 for gunpowder, rum, and fish hooks. The other reason for the name is much more intriguing. The local tradition states that the name comes from the glistening iron pyrite that is prevalent on the island. It is hard not to wonder if people looking for the pyrite gold, which is found here, ended up searching for pirate gold instead. After all, it would be easy to get the words mixed up.

The island is supposedly named for the buried treasure that consists of a chest of gold and jewels that are buried under a huge flat rock in a shallow cove on the southern point of the island—by no other than Captain Kidd himself. When one is seeking for treasure on old maps, due to spelling errors in the past, this island is also called *Juells Island*. As an interesting side note, the southern shore of this island is slowly being washed away by the Atlantic Ocean today, so the treasure may be on the ocean bottom.

Legends of buried treasure on this island have existed since the Revolutionary War era. This island has a deep landlocked harbor, with hidden caves and thick woods. Drowned forests have been found just off the shores of this island. At one time, in the Cenozoic era, this place was the top of a land mass, and not an island at all. Ancient rivers eroded the land area and the sea rushed in to fill that void, thus creating the island.

All the places on the island make a great shelter from any one observing from the sea. It is a great place for pirates to hide their ships and treasures from prying eyes. People have looked for treasure on this island for over two hundred years.

This island is two hundred and twenty-two acres and is considered an outer island on the boundaries of Casco Bay. There have been so called treasure markers found on the island. Treasure markers are piles of flat stones lain one on top of the other, until the marker reaches a height of four or five feet. Supposedly, it is near these markers that a treasure was buried.

This island is also one place where protective spirits guard the treasures buried here. Supernatural pirate ghosts, pigs, and black dogs roam this place mainly to scare any treasure seekers away. Also, loud voices cry out for help during storms, allegedly to lead the seekers away from the treasure. To get around this obstacle, a treasure seeker would need to slaughter a lamb and scatter the blood in a circle on the area where one planned to dig to appease the guardian spirits. Charms could also be used to find treasure. One seeker brought a girl and a mesmerist to the island to put the girl under a hypnotic spell on the island, so she could find the treasure. No treasure was reported as being discovered.

According to the legend, Captain Kidd was purportedly frightened toward Jewell Island by the sight of a frigate sail and buried the richest of his loot, which included gold, silver, and jewels in a large copper kettle or in a wooden chest that was taken from his ship. He buried the treasure on the southern part of the island with the help of all his crew. This is the same part of the island that is slipping into the sea. It is said that it took all of the crew's strength to place the flat rock on the treasure. Supposedly, there is an etched compass of where the treasure is on the rock with the north indicator pointing south.

Army officers, who were exploring the bay for suitable sites for forts just after the Revolutionary War, are said to have stated that Jewell Island was "a beautiful island over against the sea where the pirate Kydd, if one may believe the popular report, buried a store of jewels and other goods of rare value."

Though it is literally impossible for Kidd to have buried as much pirate treasure as is claimed, it is also true that not all of Kidd's loot has ever been found. It has to be *somewhere*. There are some interesting points to this story, however, even if it was not Kidd who buried treasure here—perhaps one of the numerous pirates who prowled the coast actually did.

Another story of a buried treasure is that in the late nineteenth century, a stranger came to the island. He was said to wear a gold or silver earring in one ear, a beaver stovepipe hat, and always carried an accordion strapped to his back. He said that he believed that the accordion was a divining instrument and would help him in his quest to find treasure. He also carried a string bag around his shoulder that was said to contain a map. The man said that his name was Willows and that the map he carried was none other then one of Kidd's treasure maps. The only thing he lacked to find the treasure on his own was a compass. He was willing to share the loot, if he could use someone's compass.

Captain Frederick or Jonathan Chase—there are two different names with the story—a known privateer, agreed to lend him a compass. It is said that when the two men got to the spot where the treasure was buried, the accordion would sustain a long low note until they started to dig in the right spot.

The two men went into the woods together, and every once in a while the island residents would hear the accordion's wheezing notes. At 11:00 pm, on only the second night of their search, the residents thought they heard a monotonous note pierce the silence of the dark. In the morning, the resident awoke to find that Chase had left on a long sea voyage and Willows apparently returned to Portland, Maine. The authorities looked for Willows, but they never found him, though they found a freshly dug pit on a remote corner of the island and the track of a rectangular object dragged through the sand to the edge of the water.

Many years passed, and Chase returned, very rich and respected in the community. His house was a show place on the island, and when he died, he was buried in his garden circled by birch trees. There was a bad storm one day after he died, and someone who was picking berries or hunting, looked to where Kidd's old pirate pit was suppose to be, and suddenly saw a cave that had never been noticed before. The person entered the cave, and found a skeleton with a gold earring and a beaver hat still on its skull.

The residents searched Chase's home and found secret passage ways, and at the end of a damp and dark tunnel, they found an old treasure map and a corroded accordion. It was too late to accuse Chase, but perhaps the islanders decided to impose a sort of justice on their own. They buried Willows and the accordion right next to Chase.

The treasure is believed to be found, and partially spent, by Chase, but perhaps he buried part of it on Jewell Island. Just to add a bit more mystery to the whole matter, there was a human skull unearthed on Jewell Island by some residents who were building a barn, but no one knows who it was.

Another twist to this legend is that a man came to the island from Nova Scotia, Canada, wearing a silver ring. He was looking for Jonathan Chase, a man who he claimed was a pirate. This man disappeared suddenly, and after Chase died, residents found a rectangular hole in a southeastern shore beach. It appears that someone dug something up in the location. Years passed, again after Chase died, the residents found a body near the treasure pit of a man who was murdered. Since then, strange sounds and mysterious lights have been seen at the treasure pit after nightfall.

To add even more mystery to this story, the island was used as a fishing station and two times, once in 1678 and in 1688, it was used as a refuge for the settlers from the mainland from Native American attacks. It was largely uninhabited except for those two times. It could be that Chase's treasure, if he found any at all, may have come from the ship of a Bermuda pirate that struck a reef called the Brown Cow, just off the island, in a storm and was wrecked during this period. Some of the crew is said to have made it to the island in a small boat. They managed to save a chest of gold, which they buried somewhere near the area called the Punch Bowl Cove. The description was very vague, and it is also said that these pirates returned years later. Chase always claimed that he entertained these suspicious visitors, and that he found a square hole on the beach of Punch Bowl Cove.

Another pirate, Ann Bonney, is said to have visited the island to bury her treasure. She and seven crewmembers buried the gold, and she shot all seven men to keep the secret of where the treasure was buried, and to guard the treasure forever. In the early 1960s, seven graves with small-unlettered markers were found on the island. Some have said that perhaps they were the graves of those crewmen.

There is also a story that during World War II, the army fortified the island, and that there are ghosts of soldiers that roamed, and perhaps still guard, this place by walking in and out of the tunnel at the southern end of the island.

Perhaps it is a combination of all these stories that is the true story of what happened on Jewell Island those many years ago. It also appears that the part of the island where all the ghosts and treasures reside is slipping into the ocean for some unknown reason. That might be the best way to keep treasure hidden forever.

Heart Island

Heart Island, once known as Dow Island, also has a legend that Kidd buried a treasure there. He supposedly buried the treasure under two basswood trees that he planted there himself. There are plenty of basswood trees on the island, just to make the hunt much more difficult, but no treasure or map has ever been found. It also seems implausible that Kidd, or any pirate, would take the time to plant trees while burying treasure.

Richmond Island

In 1855, just offshore of this island, Richard Hanscom, a tenant farmer who was plowing his fields—or it may have been his twelve-year-old son, the reports vary—found vast treasures of Spanish gold and silver coins in an earthen pot, just south of Cape Elizabeth, valued at $80,000. The pot resembled a globe lantern. Twenty-one gold coins were found on one side of the pot and thirty-one silver coins were found on the other side. In the middle was what looked like a wedding ring. The oldest coin was dated 1564. Legends say that the ring and coins may have been part of pirate Dixie Bull's lost loot.

Whoever left it here, it is obvious that the treasure was from a wreck that was unclaimed and undiscovered until that time. Many ships were wrecked off this island, so it may not be such a surprising find. There are still three ships that are said to have treasure on them that were wrecked off this island that have never been discovered. In 1864, the *Bohemian*, a steamer, was wrecked here. In 1885, the *Australia* was lost, but the lighthouse keeper, Marcus A. Hanna, rescued two of the crew. In 1916, the *Bay State*, another steamer, was lost near this island.

Bailey's Island

This island was named for Deacon Timothy Bailey, a settler who lived there in the mid-1700s. This island is unique because not only is there supposed to be another of Kidd's treasure buried on it, but part of it (but not all), has been found. Of course, it has also been said that Ned Low buried treasure here. There can be no doubt that these pirates enjoyed the northern New England area.

In 1840 or 1850, Captain John Wilson found a treasure on one of the seven rocky reefs around the island called Cedar Ledges. The treasure was lying east of Ram Island and Elm Island and southeast of Orr's Island. He was out walking, or hunting birds, on Thanksgiving Day morning or in the winter—it depends on which story one hears—on this island, when he fell into a hole. He found three caches of silver coins in the hole worth about $16,000, or he found a kettle filled with Spanish gold coins or Spanish doubloons worth around $12,000 at the bottom of the hole.

Whatever he found, it is said that he disappeared for about a month after his visit to Bailey's Island without saying a word to anyone. When he returned, he was the sole owner of a fully-rigged sloop. He even had enough money to buy a farm. The big question of the day was: Where did he get the money to buy all these things? He was well liked by the residents, but it was known that he did not save money, so the residents started to ask questions.

The true story eventually emerged. While Wilson was out hunting one day on Bailey's Island, his foot slipped into a hole. The hole looked strange to Wilson, so he took out the seaweed and found a corroded copper kettle filled with strange looking gold coins. He quickly went to Boston and exchanged the Spanish coins for $12,000. It is said that if the seeker were to go to the Cedar Ledges at low tide, they could put their hand into the hold where the treasure was found. Whatever really happened, this person who had no money, suddenly appeared with lots of money, or at least enough to buy a ship and a farm within a month.

An interesting ghost pirate story starts on Bailey's Island in Casco Bay. There is a mysterious roadway near the Nubble, which is known as the "beat of the headless pirate." This ghost is only seen during the winter months, usually around Christmas time. The apparition has no head and rides a white horse with wings up and down the road. It is said that he is guarding the rest of the pirate treasure that has not yet been found.

Cliff Island

This island is in Cumberland County, Maine, and supposedly has $400,000 buried somewhere on it. The pirate associated with this island is very different from the others we have talked about so far.

Cliff Island was originally called Crotch Island because there is a crotch on the southeastern side of the island that the resident pirate, Keiff, lived near. The island is shaped like an *H*. The H-shaped chasm on the southeast side of the island is made out of solid ledge and there are coves on each side of the crotch. Caves are found on both sides of the chasm, and legend states that treasure may hide there. The island has great coves, low sand bars, and lush pine groves. This is a great island to hide something on.

Captain Keiff or Keif, as his name is sometimes spelled, was a smuggler and a one-time pirate in his early life, but he discovered a much easier way to make a living—having the ships come to him, instead of him having to look for the ships.

The legend states that on stormy nights, Keiff would hang a lantern around his horses' neck, and ride up and down the road, luring any passing vessels into the narrow and shallow channel of the island. The light would be shone over the cliffs, when the lone cedar tress still grew there. The passing ship's crew would be misguided by the light and would wreck on the island. The reefs and ledges around the island would easily wreck any ship caught in them. If there were any crew left alive, Keiff would kill them and then plunder the ship. If any crew bodies washed on shore, Keiff would bury them with any crewmembers he had killed, in an area called *Keiff's Garden*. This was a grassy knoll, which rose above the island road that turned out to the crotch.

Keiff was supposedly helped with this type of life by none other then Captain Chase of the Jewell Island fame. Keiff and Chase were bad characters, and were famous go-betweens for smugglers. Chase's headquarters on Cliff Island allegedly perched high on the crest of the hill, with a view of the cove, called Smuggler's Cove, at the northern end of the island. Basically, the pair smuggled rum and silks. This is possibly true, because on the woody crest of the island, an iron-bound sea chest full of decayed silk was found, after both Keiff and Chase died. The house stood on the hill until 1913 when it was burned to the ground.

Visitors were not welcome on the island while Keiff lived there, but the really strange part of the story came after he died. The residents searched his house and body, but found nothing. All that treasure that he took from so many ships must have gone somewhere. He did not leave the island very often, and usually, when he did leave, he did not carry much luggage with him. One interesting theory put forward by the author of this book is that perhaps Keiff's Garden is much more then a burial site for unsuspecting victims of Keiff's schemes. If it were known that this was a graveyard, it may have kept most people from digging there.

It has also been reported that Keiff's ghost still walks the shoreline of this island. Perhaps Keiff is still trying to lure ships to the island to plunder, or maybe he is guarding the secret of his hidden treasure.

Orr's Island

This island may hide some of Ned Low's buried treasure. The story on this island is that on some nights, two men are seen carrying a heavy chest between them, and meeting a third man. There is usually a loud gasp or yell, and the third man is seen to crumple backward on the rocks, disappearing out of sight. The other two men leave the island and are not seen again.

Who they are or what they were burying is unclear and is never explained. Also, any treasure seekers are chased away by a ghost with a pickaxe, when they search for what the men were burying. Apparently, there is an enchanted treasure here. The ghosts of people or animals are said to guard enchanted treasures. Usually, the people who were burying the treasure sacrificed them to guard the treasure, until they could return to retrieve their loot.

The only strange deaths that were reported on this island comes from colonial times. At that time, this island was used as a pasture for hogs and sheep, which would attract wolves. The packs would cross the ice in the winter to eat.

It is said that John Wilson built a home near Lovell's Cove. One day, he left to hunt, but never returned home. Later that night, his wife heard shots, took another gun, and went to search for him. She also did not return. In the morning, a servant and their son rowed to another island to get help. The rescue party found the skeleton of a man and woman picked clean. There were also carcasses of wolves all over the place. Apparently, a large pack of wolves came to the island over the ice, and were held off as long as possible by Wilson and his wife for as long as their ammunition lasted.

Grand Manan Island

Six miles off Quoddy Point in Maine, there is a place called Grand Manan Island. On September 2, 1821, this island was the beginning of a story about a haunted treasure. The story started with a dream or vision of a woman named Hunt, who was living on Campobello Island at the time. Her husband was lost at sea, and she had been alone for three years at the time she had the dream.

The dream started horribly as a skinned and headless boy suddenly appeared to her. The boy told her to go to Grand Manan Island. There she would find a place called Money Cove. She would have to bring a compass, and she would see a rich treasure of gold, if she would go into the woods alone and not look behind her. Once she was in the woods, she would find a beaten path that went over the hills on a southeast course. When she went 500 feet, the boy would be waiting for her to take her to the buried treasure. The chest held $36,000 in silver, and $300,000 in gold. When they finally reached the location, a great wind would arise, but that she must not be frightened, and the treasure would be hers.

To say the least, the woman was terrified and decided not to pay attention to the dream, until it happened for three nights in a row. At that point, she knew she could not ignore the dream anymore, so she decided that she should pay attention and do what the ghost wanted. If she did, perhaps the boy would leave her alone.

So, on September 6, 1821, Hunt and four men went to the Island, landing at Whale Cove. At 10:00 pm, they headed to Money Cove. Though she was terrified, Hunt entered the woods alone. She said she saw a bright light, and in the middle was the headless boy sitting on the treasure chest. The wind picked up all around her almost to hurricane force. All of a sudden, an army of one hundred men appeared around her, crowding in on her. She screamed and fainted, awakening in the boat. The other treasure hunters found her lying on the ground, and had brought her back to the boat. They also said that they never felt fierce wind, nor saw any other people in the woods. Hunt never saw the boy again, and never returned to look for the treasure.

In 1859, Samuel Alcott Ward from Lewiston, Maine, heard the above story. He rowed to the island, and started to search for the treasure. This was obviously not an easy task, but in 1869, he suddenly disappeared off the island. His suitcase had also disappeared. He left in the middle of the night, and all that the residents found was a hole in the ground where Ward had supposedly dug.

It is believed that something iron was in the hole because there was rust found on the sides of the opening. Ward was never seen or heard from again, so the mystery of what he may or may not have found remains. An interesting side note was that the famous *Saxby Gale*, with hurricane force winds, was experienced on this very island on September 6, 1869, exactly forty-eight years after Hunt's terrifying experience.

Kennebec River

The Kennebec River was the road and lifeline between the endless trees in early Maine history. It was the best route from the interior of Maine to the coast. The river is one hundred and thirty-eight miles long; it is also the place where a great pirate treasure remains.

Richard Kennedy was the first mate to the pirate Bartholomew Roberts. Hoping to spare his own life, and also getting fifteen percent of the value of the treasure, he went to the authorities after Roberts was killed, offering to show them where the pirate buried his treasure. In 1722, the authorities decided that it was worth letting Kennedy go free to find Roberts stolen bounty, so they agreed to his terms. Kennedy kept his end of the bargain, received a fortune in finders fees, plus a large gold crucifix studded with twelve large diamonds that was worn by Roberts himself. This crucifix was thought to be stolen from a Catholic mission in Mexico. Roberts got this piece when he plundered a Spanish treasure ship returning to Spain.

To get away from his past, and perhaps trying to hide from other pirates, who may not have appreciated Kennedy helping the authorities, he moved to Boothbay Harbor, Maine, which was considered the frontier at that time. He knew that he needed a place to hide his vast fortune, so he looked for the perfect place, and found it when sailing up the Kennebec River.

He made sure that he had enough money to last a couple of years, and buried the rest of his loot in four chests on a tree-lined hill that overlooked the river. He buried the chests, four feet deep, and placed two large flat stones in the hole before filling them in. He took a piece of bark off a birch tree, and drew himself a map before returning to Boothbay Harbor. When he got home, he re-drew the map on calfskin, hoping it would keep better, and placed that map in his sea chest.

Eventually, Kennedy returned to England and bought a tavern, taking his sea chest with him. Kennedy had a hard time keeping out of the violence of his past, and he often beat up women when he was drunk. Ultimately, he was arrested and executed. He never returned to the Kennebec River area or his treasure.

Though Kennedy's chest was opened, apparently, no one could tell what area the treasure map alluded to in England. They knew that a treasure existed, but no one searched for the treasure for many years. The map came into the possession of George Benner in 1900. Benner recognized the Kennebec River area on the map, and decided to search for the loot. The map read:

"Stand abreast Qurtsbolder

Bring top in line with hill N 1/2 mile

It lise 12 fathom N.E.

Near big trees under stone"

When Benner found a large granite stone with quartz, he knew he'd found the treasure. He and a friend searched within one half a mile of the boulder, and found a low hill with one tree on it. They found the trunks of many other trees, but all the trees were dead. It was obvious that there was once a stand of trees here. Searching around the area, two treasure chests filled with gold coins and the golden crucifix were found. They knew they had located Kennedy's treasure. The men took everything from the chests, believing that was all the treasure. Kennedy said he buried four chests, but they did not find the other two chests anywhere.

The granite boulder is gone today, and the Kennebec River Valley area has changed greatly since 1900, but there are still two treasure chests buried somewhere along that river.

This is a story about a successful treasure hunt, but that is not always the case when following a map. Kennedy needed his map to be very accurate because he did not know the area at all. The treasure seeker must realize that many people were illiterate in times of old, and spelling was not usually correct. Remember that a million dollars worth of gold can occupy a space scarcely larger than an ordinary steamer trunk. However, treasure hunting is always a gamble, and the thrill and excitement of the hunt usually outweighs all other things.

The prior story proves that there may be treasure buried along the shores of the Kennebec River, and there is another place that leads one to wonder if more happened along this river than we may ever know. As discussed in an earlier chapter, this area may be what the lost Native American tribe called Norumbega Backcountry. There may be lost treasure here, in some form, but it may not be easy to recognize.

Albion is a quiet town found in the Kennebec Valley region. The town has two unsolved mysteries that somehow leads one to ponder who were the first people to live in or explore this state, and whether it was possible that they did leave behind some sort of treasure.

The first mystery lies on the lower end of a ledge rock on the Bog Road in town. The rock is weather beaten and huge, proof that it has been there a long while. The rock has the letters "J. T. A. 16.08" with an arrow pointing in the direction of the Kennebec River carved on it. The letters and arrow are covered with moss today, and one would have to dig through to find the carvings, but they are there.

The mystery is the answer to the question: What do these markings mean? No one has ever found any record of why these marks are there or what they may signify. There have been numerous explanations put forth about the origin of the carvings, and some of the theories lead to magical places or to perhaps buried treasure.

The known facts in this mystery are as follows. It is known that these carvings were there at least in the mid-1800s, most likely much earlier. The other strange fact is that until the eighteenth century, most people did not use middle initials. The reason this is strange is because most people believe that the carving 16.08 is the year date 1608, though why the dot is in the middle is a mystery. It is possible that the dot is just a spot in the rock that looks like a dot and should not be considered part of the message.

So, if an explorer was passing through here in 1608, and was marking his passage to the Kennebec River, why use the middle initial? If it is a message to unknown people passing after the explorer, then it would not matter what his middle initial was. However, if it was a message to someone who would be passing by, and the explorer did not want any misunderstanding, perhaps a middle initial would be used. Possibly, it is a joke and really does not mean anything at all. Is it a Native American sign from the lost tribe? No one knows for sure.

The second mystery again deals with people who may have visited the area, but a treasure was found that is not where one would expect to find a treasure. Some years before 1960—the exact date is not recorded—James Ridlon found an old sword at what is called "the crotch," which is a place where the Fifteen Mile River and the Bog Stream meet.

The sword is said to look ancient, but that may be just a weather worn look. Nature can be very hard on objects, so the age of the sword can not be judged on looks alone. The crest of the sword is said to have a rising or setting sun, and a woman with a reed in one hand, and a lamp in the other. Above the crest is a floral design, and on the other side of the crest is the inscription: A LA VICTORIE.

It would appear that this sword was of French origin by the inscription. But the founder did a thorough search of ancient and modern sword crests from France, and found nothing that matched what he had found simply lying in the water one day. The sword was found fairly easily. It was just lying in "the crotch," so how long it had been there is unknown. The questions of to whom it belongs, how it got into the crotch of water, and how old it is, have never been answered. Perhaps someone else unearthed it elsewhere and threw it there. Perhaps it became unearthed for some reason—a landslide or construction work—and it fell into the river, moving along slowly, until it reached the crotch and was discovered. Or maybe it was under the bottom of the crotch, and rushing water finally revealed the prize to the finder.

Whatever the answer to those questions, it is obvious that the Kennebec River Valley has some unknown treasures still hidden and are worth further exploration.

Penobscot River

All along this river's shores, numerous logging, Native American, and even Revolutionary War artifacts have been, and can be, discovered. It is what may be safeguarding these treasures that the seeker should be wary of encountering. There was much violence and death that accompanied these war relics.

It was not too long after the American Revolution had started that the colonies soon became aware that the British were not going to give up the territory easily. This was especially evident in the frontier areas. Maine was the frontier of Massachusetts at that time, and the scene of the first North American naval battle. This battle was fought on the Penobscot River and it did not end well for the Americans. There are over nineteen armed Revolutionary War ships, and over twenty transport ships that remain wrecked in the water today. Whenever battles are fought and ships are lost, there is bound to be treasure that remains behind. Over five hundred Americans died during the battle on the river that day.

On June 17, 1779, British Commander Francis McLean, landed his ship, with seven hundred British men, at what is known as Castine today. At the same time, three British sloops of war were stationed at the peninsula near the mouth of the Penobscot River. The British were building a fort there, Fort George, which still remains today, to keep the northern part of Massachusetts under their control.

The Americans did not want the British there, and even though their navy was untried, the Massachusetts Court ordered three sloops of war to the Penobscot River to get rid of the British in July 1779.

The Americans wanted to get the British out of the Castine area before they finished building the fort. They mounted an expedition known as the Bagaduce expedition, but it has also been called, the Expedition of the Penobscot. The Native American name of the river was Matchebiguatus, which means "a place with no safe harbor." That will become rather ironic, considering what was about to happen there.

This was America's first naval disaster, and historians still ague whether it was the right course of action for the court in Massachusetts to send the ships straight to the enemy. The bottom line is that they did, and there is now a wealth of historical and Revolutionary War artifacts lying on the river bottom. The relics are there directly because of the deliberate destruction of these vessels by the American crews to keep them out of British hands.

The Penobscot Expedition was fought on two fronts—the land and the sea. The land battle was commanded by Solomon Lovell. The naval battle was commanded by Dudley Saltonstall. The ships that are known to be involved in the battle are: the frigate, *Warren*, which was the flagship of the Continental navy; the brigs, *Diligent, Hazard, Defiance, Active, Pallas, Tyrannicide,* and *Hampden*; the sloops, *Providence* and *Pidgeon*; some privateer ships, *Hunter, Defence, Sally, Hector, Revenge, Putnam, Vengeance, Black Prince, Sky Rocket,* and *Samuel*.

As stated earlier, the battle went badly for the Americans. There was one bright spot, however. The first American marine landing was on Trask's Rock at Castine on the western side of the point on July 28, 1779. The bluff was 150 feet high. It was a difficult climb, and because the men had to pull themselves up by twigs and trees, they were vulnerable to enemy attack, which is exactly what happened.

Trask's Rock is a large granite boulder on the shore where the marines landed. It is said to be named for Israel Trask, a fifer who took shelter behind the rock, playing his fife while the marines made their assent. It is said that he did not lose a note of the tune he was playing during the entire assault.

As the defeat became apparent, the Americans did not want their ships to fall into the enemy hands, so they burnt and scuttled their ships right where they were. These destroyed ships can be found all along the Penobscot River. The tactic seemed to work, because the British only captured two ships, the *Hampden* and *Hunter*.

After the defeat, the British remained at Fort George until 1783. The question of why the Americans were defeated here has often arisen. It may be because of bad luck, lack of experience of the men, and poor communication issues. This theory, however, is purely speculation. The British had better communication between their troops, and were well prepared before the Americans arrived.

The present-day treasure hunter has an amazing opportunity to find Revolutionary War artifacts all through this area. It must also be noted here that most of the Penobscot River shore is privately owned, and the Penobscot River itself is considered an historic district since 1972. All finds must be reported to the state of Maine for proper excavation and retrieval.

There are some known areas where ships were scuttled by their American crews. One is the transport, *Samuel*, which was abandoned near Winterport and torched.

In 1860, William Hutchins, a native in the area, said that there were family stories that told of a brass field piece that was thrown overboard off Stover Perkin's Point. The sloop, *Providence*, was sunk near Hatch's Point, and parts of the ship were seen from the shore in 1860.

In 1975, the *Defence* was found in Stockton Harbor, which is a very cold and murky place to dive. The expedition found: cannon balls, wooden grapeshot stands, grapeshot concretion, beef bones, pieces of wood, and a bone whistle, which may have been a bos'n's pipe. One of the most unique finds from this wreck was a small box, which contained two vials. It was identified as a medicine chest from the Revolutionary War era.

Grapeshot is a small round shot that is packed in a canister that would be exploded by a fuse, so that it would not scatter until some time after the cannon projectile left the cannon.

Grapeshot is named for the fact that it was often packed in a cloth bag, rather than in a metal canister. The small balls were packed around a wooden core attached to a wood base. The cloth bag was wrapped tightly around the base. The appearance of the balls wrapped in the cloth looked like a cluster of grapes, hence the name.

In the mid-1990s, Brent Phinney, owner of a sawmill in Brewer, discovered a wooden shipwreck in shallow water just off the eastern shoreline of the Penobscot River. It is thought to be either a brig or a schooner from the fleet of the expedition. Spanish silver coins minted in 1708 have also been found there. This ship appears to be heavily armed, so it could be a naval vessel.

In 2001, an eighteenth Century cast-iron swivel gun was discovered by the Naval Historical Center Underwater Archaeology Branch. It is believed to be part of the armament of one of the ships from the Penobscot Expedition.

In 2002, the *Warren* was found in the Winterport area. It was reported to have been destroyed by the crew at Oak Point, which is Kempton Cove today.

Ten smaller crafts have been found scuttled near Bangor, just below the falls. In historical documents, this area is often referred to as the "head of navigation."

In July 2004, a wreck was found in Devereaux Cove, located one mile north of Castine, and was excavated. It is believed to be a transport ship from the fleet.

It is clear that there are still treasures to be found along the Penobscot River.

Castine Treasures

As the New England treasure hunt moves forward, it seems that there are certain places that seem to attract supernatural treasure tales more than other places. Why this is true is not known, but Castine has another haunting treasure tale to tell.

When one seeks treasure, digging, crawling, climbing, and sometimes swimming are usually the way to search for lost loot. In 1840, however, the farmer, Stephen Grindle, was hauling wood from a rocky hillside on the point at the second set of narrows on the Penobscot River, when he noticed a bit of silver shining on the ground beside him. He was about six miles from the Castine peninsula in the town of Penobscot.

Naturally very curious about the object, he picked it up. It was a silver coin, as shiny as if it had been minted the day before. When he looked at the date, he was amazed to find that it was over two hundred years old. It was then that he noticed other glints of silver all over the ground. It was almost winter and snow came early that year, so the farmer did not search to any further extent for more coins, other then the ones he had found. The next spring, he started to search again near an old Native American trail, when he found over seven hundred new coins. The actual denominations were worth well over $400. All the coins were silver.

The farmer did not mention his find to anyone for a long while. He used the coins to pay his bills, dollar for dollar. The store in town readily accepted this exchange, but the true value of this find would soon become known.

These coins were very old and priceless. They were worth much more than the $400 that Grindle used them for. In this cache, there were French ecus, Portuguese and Spanish pieces of eight, Bremen dollars, piasters and cob-money. The cob-money was extremely battered and the dates were illegible.

Cob-money is gold and silver coins made in Mexico, called maquina de papa, lote y cruz, which means *windmill* or *cross money*. They are lawful standards of money, but they look like lumps of bullion flattened and impressed by a hammer. If the date is legible, the makers usually omit the thousandth place in the date. For example, if one saw a 736 stamped on the coin, it really means the date 1736. Though cob-money was made as late as 1770, all the dates that could be read on the coins that Grindle found were minted in the 1600s.

As stated earlier, pieces of eight were made by native craftsmen who were enslaved by the Spanish. The coins were produced in Peru, Columbia, and Mexico for over three hundred years. The silver was melted, then hammered to flat irregular shapes. The currency bears the Spanish coat of arms on one side and the cross of the Catholic church on the other. These are also called doubloons and could also be made of gold. The eight signified the coins denomination in Spanish reals. The end tally of the coins was seven hundred silver coins, but on the beach opposite Fort Pentagoet, one gold piece was discovered. It is not clear if this is part of the same treasure cache or not.

There are two theories as to how the coins got to the field near Castine. In 1704, Colonel Church drove the Baron Castin, for whom the town Castine is named, and his men from Fort Pentagoet. This fort is six miles down the Penobscot River, from where Grindle found his money. It has been suggested that those coins were dropped by the men as they retreated from the Colonel. The trouble with this theory is that these coins laid on the old, but heavily used, Native American trail for over one hundred years. Is it feasible to think that no one ever saw the coins glittering on the ground? This really does not seem to fit. The farmer was not looking for anything and the coins were just laying on top of the ground. He had made this trip many times over the years. The coins were shiny; it is the glint from the sun that caught his eye in the first place, so they could not have been there very long. The next guess would be that the river must have flooded and washed these coins on shore shortly before he found them. There is no documentation of the river flooding at this time, but it may have had some minor flooding. There is, however, a second, and much more intriguing theory.

The Baron Castin's daughter and grandchild were also in the Fort when it was attacked by Colonel Church in 1704. She knew that it may be only a matter of time before she was taken captive, so she took her child and literally ran for her life. It is said that she carried a large and apparently heavy box or tin with her. This object supposedly held over two thousand coins made from silver and gold. These coins came from France, New England, Mexico, Lima, Bogota, Potois, Holland, Portugal, and England. The New England coins may have been the Pine Tree Shilling.

The Baron's daughter allegedly hid the treasure chest behind a rock near the river right before she was captured by the British. What is not so clear was if she buried the box, or just placed the box behind the rock. It is also not so clear how much time she had before the British caught up to her. That box may have broken open, disintegrated, or partially opened and some of the coins may have escaped, just floating down the rushing river. There the coins remained, just lying on the bottom, until a flood occurred a century later, powerful enough to pick up the coins, and wash them up on the old Native American trail, just before a farmer appeared with a load of wood. To Grindle, it was not a bad day's pay for hauling a load of wood to the river.

It is speculated that there are more coins to be found in the area. There may be more treasure that is not even documented hidden by the Americans from the British there. There are subterranean passages and openings that are found at the shore of the river near the Fort. Why they exist and who dug for them are unknown today.

So ends the treasure hunt on the islands and coast of northern New England. There could be many other treasures still to be found and mysterious stories to be told, but there is hidden loot still to be discovered in the higher regions of northern New England. The mountains of this area, especially the White Mountains of New Hampshire and the Green Mountain of Vermont, have their own treasure and ghost stories to be told. The quest for the higher hidden treasures and ghostly spirits begins in the very next chapter.

Chapter Eleven
Appalachian Mountain Treasures

The northern New England mountains are indeed wonders to behold. These mountains completely awed the first settlers and explorers to New England. In the Paleozoic Era, the mountains that were to become the Appalachian Chain were first folded by the violent Earth, and the seeds of the valuable gemstones and minerals that would be found were planted. A number of of the gems found here are considered some of the most unique finds in the world. When humans first reached the mountains, they soon found that they were marvelous hiding places for their own treasures. The legends and stories of these high places will take the seeker on a journey that started when the Earth's surface was still being formed.

The process of mountain building is relatively simple. It is a collision of massive continental plates in the Earth's outer layer. The force of that collision thrusts the floor up through the continent and a mountain is created.

At one time the entire land of Earth was connected as one super continent called Pangaea, which is Greek for "all lands." The super continent started to break apart and land masses floated away from each other, creating the seven known continents today. This is not a permanent condition; nothing on Earth stays the same forever, it is always changing.

It is that force that keeps the planet alive, and two hundred million years from now, the continents will once again come together to be a new super continent, called Neopangaea or "New all lands."

There is a basalt layer under the Earth's crust and a granite layer over all the land masses. This means that the continents "float" on a basaltic layer and the mountains "float" on the granite layer. Like an iceberg or island, most of the mountain lies beneath the surface of the Earth. Only the top is exposed. It has been thought that the mountains "floating" along the top of the continents also respond to the gravitational pull of the moon—like the tides—and that they actually gently rise and fall as much as six inches per day.

One fourth of all land areas are mountains or mountainous, meaning that they are at least 3,000 feet in altitude. There are dead volcanic mountains in New England; for example, Mount Ascutney in Vermont, had a very eruptive origin, and Burnt Meadow Mountain in Brownfield, Maine, is an extinct volcano. There are also two extinct volcanoes in Aroostook County in Maine. The Monadnock mountains here, are mountains that rise conspicuously and solidarity above a surrounding peneplain or countryside. A peneplain is a flat, unrelieved plain that is the end product of the erosion of land.

In many respects, the Appalachian Mountains are very mysterious. The Appalachian relief height, which is the height from its top to its bottom, is about the same as the Rockies. These mountains are just large piles of broken mass or earth piled up together. It has also been theorized that the Appalachian Mountains have uplifted and eroded away at least three times, since they were first created. In the past, the mountains have looked like how the Rocky Mountains look today, and in the future, the mountains will look like how the plains of Kansas look today.

The Appalachian chain is a product of a horizontal thrusting, in which the crustal material was carried from great distances and thrown upward. The mountains are a folded mountain range, which means that the bending of strata and layers of rock actually created the mountains. These mountains consist of a double belt, with the inner belt compressed under the outer belt. To accommodate the forces exerted on the rock, the mountains dislocate and crumble, constantly building upon itself. As the mountains rise, they also fold over, which creates incredible pressure within the rock. The rock within the mountain is compressed, melted, and metamorphosed into other forms of rock by the pressure of the folding process. This is why there are so many precious gemstones found here.

Sometimes the folding process can be very severe, causing loops and hairpin curves when they topple over and turn upside down. Usually, the folding causes the ridges in the mountains and the valleys down below. One of the most amazing aspects of the folding here is that it is accomplished while the rocks are not in a liquid form. One tends to think of rock as solid, never moving an inch, but it will gradually bend under this type of pressure. It will also break, which will eventually cause a fault in the rock.

What tends to be interesting about the Appalachian chain is that it has some rocks that have been overthrusted faulted.

That means that while the bending and folding of rocks occurred, some of the older rocks were bent over the younger rocks. Now, the older rocks sit on top of the younger rocks in the mountain.

Parts of the folded mountain created the mountain root, and the rest is thrust up through the continental plate. This process helps to explain why there are marine fossils found high in mountain areas. The other reason is that before the plates collided, they must have been separated, which is called a rift. A sea is usually between the plates at that time. As the floor of the sea is pushed up, the marine fossils become lodged in the mountaintops.

The Appalachian Mountains are made of resistant igneous and metamorphic rock. Igneous rocks are rocks that once existed in a molten state that were melted at a very high temperature. Metamorphic rocks are any kind of rocks that have been altered by a high temperature and pressure. This creates new types of minerals, textures, and gemstones. For example, Vermont marble is a metamorphosed limestone. This is another of the reasons for the variety of gemstones and minerals found in these mountains.

The Native Americans who lived here worshiped the mountains of the area. They could tell that the mountains created the weather in the land below, and decided that they should leave well enough alone. They did not want to anger, bother, or intrude in the lives of the spirits who were living on the mountain top. This was the main reason that they did not climb the mountains or would only climb to a certain level. The mountains were a mysterious place, with ghosts, Gods, and spirits occupying that realm. The Native Americans were very superstitious of the high places and would not name the mountains or even talk about them. The Native American population did not give any of the Native American names that the mountains may now have today. When the settlers came to New England, they wanted landmarks to help them find their way around. The mountain was the easiest landmark to see. If the settlers named the mountains with a Native American name, it was usually the name of a waterway or village nearby, or it was the basis of a Native American legend of that area.

In spite of the fact that the Native Americans did not climb the mountains, they were excellent miners. They just did not go above a certain altitude. They were mining the elements of the area long before the first settlers came. In the beginning, the Native Americans would tell the settlers where the mines were, which is why the settlers continued to mine the area well into the 1800s.

When the settlers started to torture the native people or enslave them to work the mines, the secret of where many of these mines were went to the graves with the Native American people. It did not matter what was done to the Native American people, they would not tell their secret, and would kill their own, if others told the settlers where the mines were located.

The Native Americans were also great gem miners. Some of the old mines have been discovered, but many are still unknown, especially the jadeite and nephrite jade mines that are said to exist somewhere in the mountains. The first gem mining company formed in North America was in New England in 1880.

Yellow Ore!

Gold! That element is the most searched after metal in the world. There are physical reasons that this is true. Gold usually survives as nuggets, because the nature of gold is very malleable and permits the metal to survive water pounding without disintegration. The golden metallic sheen mesmerizes people when it is cut and it can be hammered without shattering the metal. Gold and silver are arborescent elements, which means that they grow "tree-like," in veins, the way a tree would grow branches.

Gold also comes in various colors. If is has a greenish hue, it has a high percentage of cadmium embedded. A reddish hue indicates that it has a high copper content embedded. If is has a whitish hue, it has silver or platinum, or perhaps both, in it. A bluish hue is a sign that it has a high iron concentration.

One thing to remember when searching for gold is that it is nearly insoluble, but is often found with soluble sulfide minerals, which can affect plant growth. What that means to the treasure seeker is that an absence of plants or stunted plant growth may indicate a highly mineralized vein underground.

Mining is not just a new world enterprise. In Bulgaria, treasure seekers have found solid gold artifacts, which are six thousand years old. It seems that people could mine and purify gold at that time. Egypt is where the first underground mines were found. Some of the mines there were 300 feet deep. The Egyptians would make a fire in the ground, then quickly put out the fire with cold water, and create fissures. Then, they would use picks to crack open the ground.

Of all the gold ever found, ninety percent of the metal has been found since 1848. The main reason is because all the placer or surface gold was found before 1851. To find more gold, the miners had to go underground. Placer gold is a western term of Spanish origin for deposits containing gold particles that were obtained by washing the gold out of the dirt.

Of course, seeking placer gold was not as easy as it may have sounded. Just looking for gold nuggets in the flowing rivers could not be that difficult, one would assume. That just was not the case at all. The first problem for the seeker was that one could only look for gold at certain times of the year, not whenever one wanted to. The water volume had to be high and swift enough to wash away gravel and sand. That usually meant that panning for gold took place in the spring of the year. The water was usually ice cold, because of snowmelt, and a gold seeker would pan twelve to fifteen hours per day, seven days a week. He—and it was men who would usually search for the gold—worked in a bent over position, shoveling huge amounts of dirt for three to four months per year.

Golden nuggets are not found very often today. In forty tons of ore, a miner today may only find one ounce of gold. Though technology has improved the life of an underground miner, there are still dangers that can not be controlled by man. There are cave-ins, poisonous gas, and spontaneous rock explosions, called rock bursts, that kill miners to this day.

So, the first part of this journey in seeking lost treasure in the mountains of New England will take place in the Longfellow or Blue Mountains of Maine.

After all, the quest for gold and other gemstones does not wait for anyone. The spirits guarding the treasures have no where else to go, and are anxiously awaiting the next seeker.

Chapter Twelve
Longfellow Mountains
of Maine Treasures

It would seem that a Maine resident would not have to go to California to dig for gold when the Gold Rush began. Prior to the 1849 Gold Rush era, there were hints and rumors that a solid gold wall was hidden somewhere in the Moose River Valley in Maine. Apparently, it was just sitting there, waiting for someone to chip off the pieces, and take them to market. This may be part of the tale that Champlain heard about Norumbega, but unlike the tellers of Champlain's tale, there is an interesting history regarding what happened in the Moose River Valley that lends a touch of truth to this tale.

Samuel Berry, a resident during the years prior to the Gold Rush era, had an unusual habit of disappearing for a few weeks, and then returning with just enough gold to see him through for a short period of time. He would not tell a soul where he was going or how he got this raw material whenever he wanted or needed it. When the Gold Rush did start, Samuel decided he would go to California, not to dig for gold, but to learn the finer points of gold digging from the miners there. Before he left, his friends begged him to tell them his secret, in case he never returned. Samuel refused, and left by ship around Cape Horn. As happened with many of those gold field bound ships, it was lost at sea, and Samuel was never seen or heard from again.

This should be the end of the story of the wall of gold, but there was an old newspaper article written around 1890—the name of the newspaper is not reported—that continues the story. On the morning that Samuel left, he did break down and tell a friend the location of the gold. The friend made several trips to the area, and returned with several pieces of gold, which he sold in Augusta. One day, he just stopped mining with no real explanation.

So, here ends the story of the missing wall of gold. Perhaps there is a solid vein of gold that still exists somewhere in the Moose River Valley. Perhaps the tellers of Champlain's tale just did not give the correct directions.

What Happened Here?

That is not the only strange story to come from the Moose River Valley. It seems that where treasure tales exist, there is usually a mysterious death story soon to follow. Mitchel B. Kaufman, a hunter from Massachusetts, disappeared into this region's forest around the Crocker Pond Camp area on November 4, 1930. This disappearance began the largest manhunt the area had ever seen up to that point.

A group of hunters, with two guides, made plans for the group to meet at an appointed place and time. The group separated and Kaufman never made it back to the area where he was suppose to meet his companions. At first, the group thought that Kaufman was in hot pursuit of game, and really did not worry much. He was dressed appropriately for Maine's late fall weather, and he carried a rifle with plenty of ammunition. It was not so cold that he would not survive the night sleeping outside. Besides, his friends said that he was an experienced outdoorsman.

Four days passed, and over fifty experienced woodsmen searched the area for him, but found absolutely nothing. There was no sign of Kaufman. A five hundred dollar reward was offered to induce more volunteers to help the search. Footprints were found about a quarter of a mile from camp, but lead the searchers nowhere.

Several theories cropped up as to what might have happened. One theory was that he was hot on the trail of a deer, and lost his way. Another theory was that he was shot by another hunter and he was buried to hide the crime. Still another theory was that he committed suicide, and even foul play was mentioned. None of these theories stood up under close examination, and no unexplained gun shots were reported.

On November 12, 1930, the first organized search was made. They searched an eighteen mile area and four search planes scoured the woods from the skies above. There was food and water in the woods for Kaufman to find and survive on, and he had a supply of chocolate with him. No trace of a fire or anything else was ever found.

Bloodhounds were brought into the search. The dogs tracked him heading on a trail toward Canada, and then to a small hut about eight miles from camp. Four miles from that camp, the searchers found dead flashlight batteries of the type that Kaufman had. At this point, they believed that Kaufman had deliberately got lost. The dogs lost his trail at a brook that Kaufman's guide told him not to cross.

The reward rose to $1,000 for any news about Kaufman. No one ever collected the money. On November 13, 1930, one thousand men searched the area for any signs of the lost hunter. Pinkerton detectives were hired by the family to investigate the entire affair. The search had tones of a murder mystery, many facts were never fully explained, and perhaps had absolutely nothing to do with the disappearance. One fact stated that there was a Jackman, Maine taxi seen in Boston by the city police four days after Kaufman was reported missing. Speculation ran rampart that Kaufman must have planned this. To this day, no one knows why that taxi was there.

On November 16, 1930, the search was officially called off. After searching six hundred square miles, nothing conclusive was ever found. On May 18, 1931, the Boston Post announced that the body of Kaufman had been found nine miles from Crocker Pond. It appears that Kaufman did die from exposure and nothing more.

The questions remain, however, as to why no trace of him was found during the extensive search? The area where he was found was searched thoroughly. Where he went, and why he did not try to help the searchers find him is still a mystery. He could have fired his rifle, made a fire, stayed in one place (like the hut he was tracked to), any and all of the above, would have helped searchers find him. Kaufman did not have a broken arm or leg, but maybe he hit his head and was delirious. No one will ever know.

The name for the state of Maine is said to have come from perhaps two sources. The first is that it was named by the English settlers in 1607 to distinguish it from the islands all along the coast. The mainland became shortened to Maine. The second thought is that the French settlers named it in 1635, after a historic province in the northwest of France, just south of Normandy. The ancient name was Cenomania from the Celtic word *Cem*, which means *hill*. The tribe living in that area was called Cenomanni or hill dwellers. The last part of that name is said to have given the present day state the name Maine.

There are thirteen mountains in Maine that are over 4,000 feet high; the tallest is Mount Katahdin reaching the height of 5,267 feet. Being the largest stand-alone mountain in New England, it is not really surprising that there are some supernatural legends about this mountain.

Legends and Beliefs

New England was settled by people who had very strong religious beliefs called the Puritans and Pilgrims. They were hearty people, and they worked very hard to settle this area. Many of their strong religious beliefs reverberate throughout the folklore and legends of the region.

There is a superstitious legend that existed during the logging days at Mount Katahdin. This legend is said to have roots in biblical times. The loggers believed that the Poplar tree was an evil tree. It is said that this was the type of tree that Christ was crucified on. It was considered bad luck to build anything with the Poplar tree by the logging industry at this time. The tree, however, did make great firewood.

One day, so the legend goes, a young logger decided to use part of the Poplar tree from a stand of Poplar that stood in the shadow of the mountain, to make a pole to steer the bateau, or the boat that was used to drive logs down the river to the mills in Bangor. During the log drive, the pole he made, snapped or split in the white water, and the bateau threw all the occupants into the raging water. All the men survived this ordeal with no major damage, except the lumberjack who made the Poplar pole. He lost his leg, and could never run logs again.

There is a stand, or group, of yellow Poplar trees at the base of Mount Katahdin. The problem is that the yellow Poplar tree does not belong to the Poplar family; it is part of the Magnolia family. These trees are called Tulip trees. The leaves and flowers have a tulip-shape or outline. The Tulip tree is one of the tallest eastern hardwoods that grew in Maine's forest. The wood is finely grained and very resistant to splitting when dry. It is mainly used for shingles, furniture, toys, and pulp. The Native Americans did use this tree to make one-trip only dugout canoes for heavy cargo.

The most interesting part of this story is that there are pieces of the legend that may be true. This tree actually does tend to break up when exposed to water for too long. It is the reason that the Native Americans used this canoe for one-time use only. Though these trees are not actual Poplar trees (and the loggers would know this), for some reason, they believed that these were the trees that were supposedly cursed. It is a good story, whether the story comes from fact or true experience, or from the imagination during the long, cold nights around the logger's campfire. It also shows a connection between the embedded religious beliefs of the area and actual experiences from New England's population.

The Longfellow or Blue Mountains of Maine are called the White Mountains in New Hampshire, but when they enter Maine, they change names and become much lower in elevation. Folding, broad upwarping and glaciation, all created the Longfellow Mountains. Originally, the Earth's crust was intensely folded. Then, it was worn down to a flat plateau. Next, came the molten rock that was intruded to form a batholith, and then the land un-warped. Finally, a glacier came along, and scoured away much of the un-warped material, leaving the surface rocks called schist, gneiss, and granite.

It also hid the gold! That yellow ore of the Earth! It does not matter if a seeker finds that substance in the tunnel of a mine or by panning a fast moving river or stream, it is the one mineral that treasure seekers all dream of finding. Though it would be nice to just have one spot where the treasure was buried, finding gold is not that easy. For example, there has been gold found in the bed of the Sandy River, but the full amount of what lies beneath has never been completely explored.

Mining

The gold mining craze struck Maine in 1880. Hundreds of mines were opened and financed at $100,000 to $500,000 each. Some of the mines did offer amazing minerals and gemstones in the soil, but many did not.

There was gold found in many locations in Maine. The list is truly amazing. Gold has been found in York County, in the Boston Fault area, though the details are vague. Below is a list of just some of the areas that gold has been found. It is not a complete list, but it will give the reader the sense of the vast gold vein that must run through Maine. Gold has been reported in: Acton, Albion, Farwell Mountain in Bethel, Augusta in the Kennebec River, Baileyville in the Saint Croix River, Baring, Calais, Carmel, Cutler, Dallas in the Nile Brook, Carabassett Valley, Carrying Place, China, Columbia, Concord, Gardiner, Goldfield, near Houlton, Haynes Township, Minot, Houghton in Brandeen Stream and Bemis Stream, Gouldsborough, Hampden, Hancock, Harmony, Harrington on Flint Island, Lubec, Moscow, Anson, Mount Vernon, New-field, New Portland, New Sharon on the Sandy River, Orland, Orrington, Betsey's Guzzle area in West Paris, South Wood-stock, Pembroke, Cole Hill Gore in Woodstock, Pittston, Saco, Sandy River Plantation, Sullivan, Verona, Strong, Dennistown, Madris, Appleton in Rock Pond, Mount Abraham Township, Magalloway, Lincolnville, and the Parmachenee area.

Today, many of these mines have been backfilled and covered, so the exact location may never be known. It is possible that many rich finds could still be made today, if the locations could be found. It has been said that a line of metal runs northeast from Lincolnville through the Blue Hill peninsula and continues across Maine. Metals in this line are gold, copper, lead, arsenic, tin, and nickel. These metals are trapped under a granite ledge in a long fracture zone that was caused by a major impact with a celestial object or by movement of tectonic plates over five million years ago.

Western Maine is the best place to search for gold today. Underground mining or panning can find this precious metal, and to this day, the mother lode in this area has never been discovered.

The men who searched for the gold in Maine in the late 1800s worked in very dangerous conditions. At any time, disaster could strike these miners. Cave-ins, suffocation, and premature dynamite explosions happened much too often. Men would do whatever they could to be as safe as possible—and that even included obeying the superstition laws.

There is a superstition about women in mines that can be traced back to Great Britain before the mid-nineteenth century. It was considered bad luck to let a woman in the mine tunnel. Even today, seventeen out of the twenty-eight mining states have laws that prohibit women from working in the mines or even entering the mine for any reason or under any circumstances.

There is an ancient legend in Maine about the lost Native American gold mine, one that is supposed to be located in the vicinity of the Lead Mountain Ponds and Lead Mountain in Hancock County. The mine supposedly exists near the town of Aurora, named after the Goddess of Dawn. There is supposed to be gold ore in those mountains, but no lost mine has ever been found.

An interesting side note to this story is that there is a stream in Hancock County called Gold Stream for the gold nuggets that were found there. It is the only stream in that county that claims to have gold in it, so perhaps the gold does flow from the old Native American gold mine. This is purely speculation, but it does make sense that the gold must come from somewhere. However, it is in western Maine, Oxford County, to be precise, that the largest gold find was made.

The nation's first gold strike was in Oxford County on the Swift River in Byron, Maine. Most of the gold here was found in the east branch of the river in pot holes, which are pockets that are worn into rocks by the action of the water. Small stones, gravel, and gold will get caught in them. It has also been found that gold seems to exist where the gemstone garnet exists. Why that is true is not really known.

The first gold here was said to have been found in a very unusual way. A farmer in the region killed one of his chickens for dinner. While he was eating, several hard gritty things were swallowed. When he pulled one out, he found tiny gold nuggets. He had moved his chicken coop to the river, and apparently there was gold dust in the crop of his chickens who had been pecking along the riverbank. The chickens were eating the gold. He quickly started to pan for gold in the area and soon found actual nuggets. It was said that gold was so plentiful here that at one time people would practice shooting their shotguns at ledges with shells filled with gold.

The Swift River in Byron and the river tributaries are thought to have produced more gold then all the other gold locations in the state of Maine. The reason that this is true is because the rocks in the river stand on the edge of the banks that catch the gold as it is swept downstream by the strong river current. Thousands of dollars have been taken out of the Swift River to this point. It is said that one prospector removed $14,000 worth of gold by panning this river over a number of years. There are stories about lumbermen who were working near the river finding gold. One employee of a lumber company is said to have found two nuggets that totaled eighty-two dollars in 1840. One nugget was worth seventy-two dollars by itself.

The largest gold nugget ever taken from the Swift River weighed 18.50 grams. It was discovered in Byron and was worn completely smooth by the river's action against it. It may have been in the river a very long time. Legend states that anyone who knows how to pan for gold, will get "color," which means *will find gold*, when the treasure hunter cleans the gravel out of a crevice in the ledges in the stream. The High Sheriff's badge of Oxford County is made from Swift River gold, as well as the Maine state necklace, which is displayed at the Maine State Museum in Augusta, the state capital.

In the book, *Gold Hunter's Guide Book*, by Jay Ellis Ransom, the exact location of the first gold strike is revealed.

"Areas along Gold Brook: (a) in Chase Stream Tract Twp: placers: (b) in T5 R6 (which means Township 5, Range 6), and Appleton Twps. numerous placers: (c) along the Smith branch of the Penobscot River, especially in Sandy Bay, Bald Mountain, and Printess Twp.—placer gold. In St. Albans, the St. Albans mine is primarily lead with gold traces."

To reach the Swift River to pan for gold today, take Route 17 at Byron, and drive north on the road for about a mile and a half until you reach the river. Park the car and take the wood road across the river. When one reaches the fork in the road, take a left, and go west for about a mile or two. There is a five hundred-foot gorge with falls, pot holes, and other unique water features. The bedrock is basically made up of phyllite with some quartzite. **Parts of the area may be privately owned, so be sure to ask permission before panning for gold here or only pan in the designated areas.**

At Nile Brook in Rangeley, there is an interesting phenomena that occurs. Nuggets of gold have been found on one side of the brook and nuggets of platinum have been found on the other side. In 1880, the State Assayer reported that a trapper, his name has been lost to history, brought in one to four ounces of gold each year that had supposedly washed up from the streams flowing into Rangeley Lake. The Assayer suggested to pan for gold on the Sandy River from Farmington to Greendale, then on to each stream on the east side of the lake. He suggested that one should continue to pan on the waters found over the ridge until one reaches the headwaters of the Kennebec River. The rock there is hard slate, but in many places on this river there are veins of quartz, which may yield small quantities of gold.

In Skowhegan, there has been a discovery of veins of quartz that have had small quantities of gold in them. One can also pan for gold in the Perham Stream in Madrid. The story is that in 1890, a prospector panned fourteen dollars per day of gold for two weeks here.

There is also gold to be found along the Black Mountain Brook near Rumford and in gold bearing mines in western Maine. In Rumford, there is an old gold mine to be found on Bean Mountain. There was a tunnel there at one time, though it is most likely covered today. To find the old mine shaft, follow the fork of the road over Zircon Brook. **Be careful, old mine shafts are dangerous and these areas may be privately owned. Always be sure to ask for permission before searching for any old tunnels or shafts and to take proper safety precautions.**

In Livermore, there was a mine called Keith Gold Mine. It was located between the North Road and the River Road, opposite an old brick house. There were two shafts that were dropped, one went 175 feet, and the other was 75 feet. The Paris Maine gold mine was called Betsey's Guzzle, though the reason why this name was given is unknown. This mine was located on the brook north of Trapp Corner. Right around the area of Mount Cutler, near Hiram, there is a mine called the Frenchman's Gold Mine. It is really a hole in the ground, more than a mine, which was dug in the side of a mountain. **Be very careful when exploring this area. There are also many well holes here.**

Gold has been found in Kennebec County in Fogg Brook near Readfield. In Waldo County, a stone mine near Knox, has produced gold with silver embedded. In Washington County, a treasure seeker could find placer gold in the St. Croix River. In Knox County, the Owl's Head Mine near South Thomaston has produced gold with silver. In Somerset County, the Kennebec River near Caratuk is said to contain gold. This is near the Native American carrying place along the Kennebec River where, with some good luck, one could pan for and perhaps find, gold.

The search for gold is extremely hard work and usually ends with a not so happy ending. However, gold is still found in the earth of Maine and the mother lode is still missing. It is reasonable to assume that there is more gold out there, because the gold has to come from somewhere. There is always the hope that with the right equipment and being in the right place at the right time, the gold source will be found.

There are legends about lead being mined in the state by the Native Americans. The locations are in Ketchum and Dixville Notch in New Hampshire. In Ketchum, it is said that the Native Americans would cut the lead out with a knife or a hatchet. The Natives would sell this lead to the American colonists who would use the lead to make bullets. There is also a secret lead producing place called, Tarratine, but the actual location is still not known. It is supposedly where the Native Americans mined lead in Aroostook County in Maine.

Magical and Haunted Water Falls

When the first Europeans first arrived in northern New England, they could not believe the raging, wild rivers that they encountered here. These fast-moving rivers were not seen in Europe. The five major rivers in Maine were the fastest, easiest, and really the only way to get around this heavily forested state. The only way to navigate these large waterways was by birch bark canoe, which was invented by the Native Americans who lived here.

These whirling rivers held supernatural treasure secrets too, and the main obstacles on these rivers were the massive, terrifying, and un-navigable waterfalls. These were also the places where the treasures were hidden. There were cursed, haunted, and deadly falls in all sixteen counties in Maine at one time. The dams that were built have somewhat calmed these mighty rivers, but the legends of the treasures that were lost, and the ghosts and curses that still exist around these magical places, still abound.

Edes Falls is found on the Crooked River in Otisfield. The first European settler to this site was named Pierce. The natural falls here were a series of small one-foot drops. At the time of the American Revolution, a feud developed in the village of Edes Mills, a town near these falls, between George Pierce and John McIntosh. The feud came to a head, when McIntosh became interested in Pierce's nineteen-year-old daughter. During a fight at the falls, Pierce is said to have struck McIntosh with a wooden mallet, killing him.

McIntosh's ghost has apparently been seen at the falls, as well as the mills that were built at the site. People have reported that it has opened mill gates and set mill machinery to operate when no one was there. The falls are a great fishing place for landlocked salmon, and the fishermen say that McIntosh's ghost still roams there. Perhaps he is guarding the treasure that is said to be on this river. The first freshwater pearls found in North America were found in the Crooked River in Maine.

Ellis Falls is located on the Ellis River in Andover. This site is considered a cascade type of falls with a twenty-five-foot drop. It is also considered a haunted site. This legend comes from Native American folklore. In the tale, the site is called Ellis Cascade. There are two young lovers who want to be together desperately. However, the Sagamore, or chief, has other plans for his daughter. He did not want to be considered unfair, so he decided to devise a contest that would decide who would be with his daughter. There was an archery contest at fifty paces. Luckily, the lover of the young princess won. The loser was very unhappy, so he stole the woman and ran into the woods. When it became obvious that there was no where to run, and he was going to be caught, he forced the girl to jump into the waterfall with him. They both were killed there. This place is said to be haunted today with these ghosts; one ghost is always trying to escape from the other. There are pure clear crystals found there that are called the "Ellis River Diamond."

Kezar falls is located on the Kezar River in a winding gorge that is thirty feet deep and forty yards long. Massive amounts of Galena, or the primary silver-bearing ore in Maine, have been found here. There have been numerous claims of a silver vein that runs through here. Gold, Tourmaline, and Sphalerite have also been found here. Sphalerite is an important ore of zinc. The name, Sphalerite, is a Greek word, meaning "treacherous rock." The name comes from the fact that miners had a difficult time telling the difference from this mineral from Galena, the silver bearing mineral. There are stories of an old Native American lead mine near these falls.

Rumford Falls is found on the Androscoggin River in Rumford. In the 1800s, this was considered the greatest cataract in New England. During that time, there were five distinct pitches, with a total drop of 163 feet. It is thought that in ancient times, the descent must have been much higher, perhaps as high as 176 feet. There are many valuable minerals found here. Sahlite was first discovered here in 1837, the first report of this mineral found in Maine. This mineral is found in iron meteorites. Yellow garnet has also been found here.

There has been death at this site, as well. In 1833, Nathan Knapp, one of the owners of the mill located there, stepped on a wall to see if it was high enough to divert water. As the thirty-foot wall of water passed over the flume, he fell to the base of the falls and was instantly killed. The place where he died is called Knapps Pitch at times.

Snow Falls is located on the Little Androscoggin River in West Paris. It is the only cursed waterfall site in Maine. These cascade falls have a total drop of eighteen feet. Salmon quartz, garnet, black tourmaline, and a forty-pound rose quartz specimen have all been discovered at the falls.

There are many abandoned mines also in this area. The famous Native American, Molly Ockett, who was part of the Pequakeet tribe, cursed this place. She was called the Androscoggin Valley's Florence Nightingale. The legend states that she was born Molly Susup in Fryeburg in the 1700s. During her travels from Andover to Paris, she wanted refuge at the inn located at the Fall site. She was refused entrance into the inn, so it is said that she cursed the innkeeper, as well as the whole settlement, saying that they would be short of life and none of their work would prosper (or their children). It is said that no businesses prospered in that exact place since, which includes inns, cabins, schools, stores, or restaurants.

There are also waterfall sites where many gems have been discovered. The swirling water moves massive amounts of earth around and exposes the gem crystals that are hiding below. The strength of the water turbulence in these areas have moved the heavy gem crystals to the shore along the river. Some of the most rare and best quality gem minerals ever found in Maine were discovered near the many waterfall sites in the state.

It is difficult to search for these gem crystals in the waterfall area. These gems were usually found on the shore after a violent storm, a flood, or during blasting in the logging era. The water is not privately owned, but the state of Maine, power companies, paper companies, or recreational associations own most of the shore line near these powerful waterfall sites today.

Mechanic Falls is located on the Little Androscoggin River in Mechanic Falls in Androscoggin County. Legends in the area state that chrysoberyl, or gray-green crystals, were once found here. Beryl is generally unknown to the public, but it is the most important gem mineral ever found. It is usually colorless, called goshenite, in its pure form, but impurities give it varied coloration. The gem color found in Maine is usually aquamarine. There is also a lost quarry in this area where black Tourmaline called Schorl is said to exist.

Brunswick Falls is located on the Androscoggin River in Brunswick in Cumberland County. Smoky quartz was found here. Quartz, in general, is said to create a high level of energy, even causing spiritual energy to increase. The Incas of Peru used quartz to build their temples because of this attribute. The variety of quartz found near Maine waterfalls is either a rose quartz, a pink to reddish pink variety, or the smoky quartz, which is a brown to gray variety. Almandine, or large garnet crystals up to twenty-five centimeters, were found here in 1958. Garnet is commonly found in highly metamorphosed rocks called pegamite rocks. It is formed under high temperatures and pressure. Garnets are usually red, but have a wide range of color. There will be more about this gemstone in a future chapter.

Dundee Falls is located on the Presumpscot River near Gorham and Standish in Cumberland County. Almandine and beryl have also been found here. These falls are drowned falls, or destroyed by the dam built here, and no longer exist. The gems, however, would still be underground in this area.

Angel Falls is located on Mountain Brook in Township D in Franklin County. Gold and Strautolite have been discovered here. Gold is often discovered at the edges of whirlpools and in the tails of eddies, which is the bottom of a rapid that is usually at the end of a waterfall. Ordinarily, gold does not travel far from its source because it is a heavy metal. Gold can only be moved when the water is running fast.

Farmington Falls is located on the Sandy River in Farmington in Franklin County. Grossular garnet has been found here.

Livermore Falls is located on the Androscoggin River. Rose quartz and beryl have been discovered here.

Coos Canyon Falls is located on the Swift River in Byron in Oxford County. These falls were once a famous site for gold panning.

Mother Walker Falls is located on the Bear River in the Grafton area, near the Maine and New Hampshire border. Sea-green chrysoberyl crystals were found here. The waterfall is in a "cave" formed between the gorge walls and a huge talus boulder.

Pondsayer Rapids is located on an unnamed stream northeast of Rangeley and Stratton in Lang Plantation in Franklin County. A four-ounce nugget of gold was found here. The story goes that lumberjack Cyrus Campbell, in 1884, was looking in this area for his lost pick pole, which is a logging device, while he was driving logs through here. He found the nugget in a crevice that was filled with yellow stones. He could only get one out and was never able to find the place again.

Step Falls is located on Wight Brook in Newry in the Step Falls Preserve. Beryl and pyrrhotite has been found here. Green and blue tourmaline gems have been found at the top of the falls.

Skowhegan Falls is located on the Kennebec River in Somerset County. A one centimeter nugget of gold was once found here. There are also legends about massive rose quartz crystals that have been found. Veins of the crystals may exist in the entire area and not just in the vicinity of the falls. The falls may have just exposed part of the vein that is near the falls. When Benedict Arnold passed these falls on his trek through Maine to Canada, he reported that they were as tall as six men. It must have been an amazing site, and it certainly intimidated the men as they portaged around the falls.

In 1957, experts claimed that a gold vein ran westerly from Veazie Falls and terminated near Stillwater on the Penobscot River. This is an unsubstantiated claim at this point.

At Ayer's Falls on the same river, a strange Native American legend exists. These falls are between Ayer's Island and Orono in a place called Nutskamongan, and it is said to be the home of the people called Wanagemeswak or dwarf people. They were the ones who foretold the coming of the Mohawk tribe to destroy the Abenaki tribe. They warned the Abenaki, so the tribe could be prepared when the Mohawks arrived. It is said that these people stayed in the woods, wearing red caps, with ears that stuck up. They were three feet high and considered very ugly.

There are many Native American tales about these remarkable people. They were usually considered benevolent, but could, however, become very mean. If they were laughed at, they were believed to possess the "evil eye." If they made direct eye contact with a human, it would result in immediate death or a fatal illness. Could they be considered the supernatural guards of some mineral treasure that may be found along the mighty Penobscot River?

Gems!

As seen in the prior paragraphs, beautiful gemstones are abundant in Maine. The smoothness of a quality gemstone has been, and can be, mined in the Maine mountains. The word *gem* conjures the cool, smooth beauty of a precious stone sliding through the hand of the discoverer. These stones are something that humans have aspired to own since the first gems were uncovered in the Earth in ancient times.

Gem lore is principally based on the symbolism of color. The unique and rich color of the object is what lures treasure seekers to search and ultimately find the gem.

There are three main virtues of a gem. The first is the color and luster, which is the effect of surface reflection off the gem. The second is the durability or hardness of the stone, and the third is the rarity of the gem that is found. Even the so-called colorless gems, like the diamond, have some aspects of color. It is called the dispersion or the fire of a gem. Dispersion is where and how the light is broken up into its component colors or spectrums.

A secondary virtue of a gem, which can make a gem more valuable, is its phenomenal or optical quality. Any gem can have a phenomenal quality. The gems that do possess this quality fall into three categories. The first is asterism, which means that the gem creates a star-like ray of light. The next category is a chatoyancy, which means that the gem has a band of light on its surface, and the last category is called dichroism, or two distinct colors which are seen at a right angle to each other in the gem.

One of the most famous gemstones, the diamond, is said to be found in Andover and Freeport, Maine, and in Colebrook, New Hampshire. Though at first glance this story may seem farfetched, it should be noted that diamonds have been found on an island in the St. Lawrence River, east of Montreal. Could diamonds have moved from that area to Maine and New Hampshire over time? There is an extinct volcano near Colebrook, New Hampshire, so perhaps the immense pressure at this place did create diamonds.

Three of the most rare gems found in New England are found in the western Maine and New Hampshire mountains. The first is the amethyst, which is the most valuable variety of quartz. Quartz is the hardest of all common minerals. A pure quartz crystal contains only silicon and oxygen. It is clear and glassy. The crystals are six-sided and are sometimes found singly or in masses.

Impurities are what give quartz its color. The lavender to royal purple color made it the gem of choice of royalty and the church hierarchy in Europe. The glass-like luster just enhances the gem and any impurity gives it a violet hue. This gem is found in areas of pegmatite mineralization, usually embedded in white or yellow kaolin, which is a clay-like substance. In eleventh century Europe, the wearer of an amethyst would instantly be cured of drunkenness, could control evil, and would quickly become intelligent. If a bear was engraved on the stone, the wearer could put demons to flight.

In the early 1920s, at Deer Hill in Stow, Maine, a six hundred-point cavity of amethyst was found. There are still pieces of the gem there. Pleasant Mountain in Denmark was another mining area for amethyst, but the area has not been fully explored or mined yet. It is considered a premier area to hunt for unknown rich finds of this gemstone.

The second gem that is found in Maine is Tourmaline. It is the gem that seems to be found only on the Atlantic and Pacific coastline of North America. In California, the tourmaline is basically yellow and in Maine, the tourmaline is basically a blue-green color. However, other colors of the gem have been discovered here. The six colors of tourmaline found in Maine are: black (schorl), brown and white (chavite), blue (indicolite), red and pink (rubellite), green (elbaite), and the colorless (achroite). The gem can be found from Byron to Woolwich. Tourmaline has been found at Mount Apatite, Mount Mica, the Harvard Mine in Greenwood, as well as the mines in Newry.

The name Tourmaline comes from the Singhalses word, *tourmai*, which means "multi-colored, water-worn pebbles." That is what tourmaline looks like when found. In 1820, two schoolboys first discovered the gem in tremendous quantities in Mount Mica in Paris, Maine.

The story starts late in the fall of 1820. Mount Mica is a mountainous ridge with gray piles of broken, blasted rocks found all around from various mining operations. Two students, Elijah L. Hamlin and Ezekeil Holmes were studying mineralology, and were looking for rocks in the area. After watching the sunset one evening, Hamlin started to go home when he caught a glimpse of green from an object on the root of an upturned tree. This was the first glimpse of the gem that would yield to the richest tourmaline discovery, and ultimately mine, in the world.

The ledge contained crystals of green and red tourmaline. Many of the most beautiful crystals were lost in the 1800s because no one really knew how valuable these gems would finally become.

The tourmaline of Mount Mica is encased in the mica. It is said that in 1871, crystals of an almost perfect transparency and absolutely pure green color, were found and documented, but careless miners broke the crystals. None of them have been preserved. So much of the tourmaline was destroyed that would have created choice gems in today's market.

In September 1882, Tiffany & Company of New York City purchased a perfect twenty-nine carat emerald green tourmaline crystal. It is one of the finest crystals of this mineral ever known. It was found on this mountain.

For the first seventy years of operation, until 1891, only one pit was opened with twenty-nine cavities. All, except two, were filled with tourmaline. A new pit was opened in May 1895, to the east of the old pit, and fifty-nine cavities were opened. Many had tourmaline, but many were also barren. Another interesting element of this story, is that Mount Mica, the richest tourmaline mine in the world, was bought from the Native Americans for one empty old iron kettle.

A rich green tourmaline gemstone was discovered in 1862 at Mount Apatite in Auburn. There has never been another location in the world that has found such a rich, deep green tourmaline.

In 1902, the Dunton Quarry in Newry, first discovered the "watermelon" tourmaline. This is red tourmaline in the middle surrounded by green tourmaline. It is a rare form of this crystal. One of the specimens found, which is ten inches long, is in the Smithsonian Institute in Washington, D.C. In 1972, the Dunton Quarry was again in the gem world news. The largest discovery of red tourmaline ever found was uncovered. There were one hundred-carat gems discovered in that find.

Tourmaline has a commercial use, as well as being considered a gemstone. It has a piezo-electric property, meaning that an electrical charge develops the instant a wafer is sliced from a crystal that is severely compressed. This is a very useful property in making high pressure gauges.

The third gem found here is garnet. The garnet is found in both Maine and New Hampshire. Garnets can come in all colors, except blue. This gem is really not a stone, but is a silicate mineral and comes from the Latin word, Granatum, which refers to the seeds of a pomegranate, which is what the gems resemble. In eleventh century Europe, if a lion was engraved on the garnet stone, the wearer would be protected and receive honor and wealth. It could cure the wearer of all disease and would guard against all perils in travel. Obviously, this is quite a gem to find and keep.

Blue Hill Copper

Blue Hill, Maine, has had its share of mining in the past. Silver, copper, gold, granite, and black tourmaline have all been found in the area. The most famous mines are copper and silver mines, though there were mines for gold, too. Three of the mines in the area were the Atlantic mine, that produced silver and copper; the Blue Hill Mine, which produced copper; and the Douglas Mine, which also produced copper.

Copper was discovered in Blue Hill in the 1870's, believe it or not, by a tourist. Parker H. Savage was a resident who left, but came back for a visit. On the day before he left for home, he found a vein of copper. He told some local residents before he left, and though it took a few years, the copper mining craze finally hit the town. The craze lasted from 1879 to 1881, and it was intense while it lasted.

The copper found in Blue Hill was called purple copper and the ore was one of the finest quality, at least according to the experts of the time. In November 1879, William Frank Stewart, called Professor Frank Stewart, became interested in the mining operations in Blue Hill. Stewart was the person who assayed an unrecognized silver ore in Nevada and declared the ore to be valuable beyond imagination. This spurred others to search the area more closely, and directly due to his assay report, the famous Comstock Lode in Nevada was discovered. It is clear that he knew what to look for when searching for valuable minerals.

Professor Stewart came to the area and surveyed Blue Hill, stating that "it could possibly be a silver bearing region, but all that glitters is not gold," he warned, but it did not stop the fever for silver from expanding. By May 1880, at least twenty-one mining companies were in operation in Blue Hill, all hoping to strike the rich vein.

No rich silver vein was ever found in the area and Stewart blamed "the lack of judgment," in part, "of the many mine managers of Maine" for that fact. He headed west shortly after he made that statement, and did not ever return to Maine.

Blue Hill never quite made it as a mining boomtown and soon the town had to search for other ways to make money. It is no secret that copper did exist in Blue Hill and it was mined successfully. Thankfully, Blue Hill did not become a mining ghost town after the copper ran dry, like so many western mining towns. The veins were not very large or extensive enough to really be profitable over an extended period of time. When the vein finally tapped out, the mining companies soon left the area. There are overgrown shafts and broken walls from the mining camps that can still be found in the Blue Hill area today, but the mining fever has finally broken.

Chapter Thirteen
White Mountains of New Hampshire Treasures

The Native American tribe of the White Mountains area were called the Pemigewasset. They called the White Mountains, Waumbek-Methna, which meant "mountains with snowy foreheads." Their word for Mount Washington was Agiocko-chook, which meant "abode of the Great Spirit" or "The place of the Great Spirit of the Forest." The Native Americans called the tallest peak, Agichooks, and this was considered the actual seat of the Great Spirit. This is also the place where the Great Spirit of the mountain sent forth the deluge that covered the entire earth. Only the top of Mount Washington remained dry. A hare was released from the top and when it brought back dry grass, it was safe for the people to descend and to start life again on earth. If this story sounds familiar, it does resemble the story of Noah's Ark from the Bible.

This Great Spirit did not like any encroachment of his territory by mere mortals. Manitou was the Great Spirit of the mountain, but he was also an evil spirit. His voice was thunder and his anger was lightning. To the Native Americans, the mountains were not worth climbing, no matter how much wealth or treasure might be there. They also saw that the mountains were snow or cloud covered a great deal of the time. It would not be a pleasant place to go. To this day, the people that do live on this mountaintop say that there is a "presence" around this place. No one can explain why he or she never feels alone there. Many hikers and climbers have died while trying to make it to the summit; perhaps they are still trying to finish their climb.

The name of New Hampshire comes from a county of Hampshire in England. Mason, the person who had the patent embracing a considerable part of the state came from this area. New Hampshire's nickname, the Granite State, came from the igneous rock that exists there. The very coarse granite stone is pink in color and the finer granite stone is black and white. The White Mountains were once a mass of molten minerals and are generally circular in shape.

These are very old mountains; they were two hundred million years old when the Rocky Mountains in the west were first formed. The vegetation that lives and survives on the mountains tends to like limestone and thrive very well in it. The winds blow almost constantly in these hills; there are gusts over one hundred miles per hour every month of the year. Mount Washington has seen the highest winds ever recorded on the Earth's surface, 231 miles per hour on April 12, 1934.

Mount Washington and Other White Mountain Treasure

Mount Washington is 6,288 feet high. In thirty million years, erosion will wear this mountain down, and Mount Washington will be on the same level as the sea. Mount Washington started to build to its present height 350 million years ago, when the sediments that made up the range were layered-down mud in shallow seas. When the mixture cooled, then granite was formed and the mountains were created.

Captain John Smith first described the White Mountains in 1614. He called Mount Washington "the twinkling mountains of Angosisco." Giovanni de Verrazano first called the mountains the Crystal Hills in 1524. It is obvious from these first explorers reports that there was something about these mountains that seemed to noticeably shine from a distance. Was it valuable gems that were glinting in the glorious sunlight, just laying there for the taking, or was it something else, perhaps not of this world, shining for all to see? That is just one of the mysteries that will be explored in this chapter.

There are Native American glyphs etched on a pine tree on the shore of the Winnipiseogee River in New Hampshire. There is a canoe with two men in it carved on the tree. This is thought to indicate a direction for anyone to follow. Is it a great fishing spot, a lost village, danger, or perhaps a lost treasure or mine? No one really knows for sure.

It is known that the Winnipiseogee tribe, Ossipee tribe, and Pigwacket tribe, all from the Fryeburg, Maine area, were very hostile and at war with each other much of the time. They used the water as a highway, so the glyphs could be anything, even conceivably a trap for another tribe to fall into. In the early 1700s, the Algonquin tribe is said to have hid a huge treasure in a cave in the Rock Rimmon area, located two miles west of Kingston. The details are vague as to what type of treasure this was.

Goldmining

There have been twenty-six gold mines and sixteen silver mines in the White Mountains. There are also lost mines in Whittier and Carroll County, New Hampshire. The mines of the White Mountains have produced many different minerals, such as: iron, copper, lead, mica, zinc, gold, silver, tin, cobalt, and garnets.

In 1866, gold was discovered in the town of Gunthwaite, now called Lisbon. This was when the excitement of mining came to the mountains. This mine was of a highly speculative nature. During the ten years of operation, one and a half million dollars was spent and absolutely no gold was taken from the area. How gold was discovered here in the first place is that J. Henry Allen was digging in David Atwood's pasture and dug up quartz crystals that contained veins of real gold.

Though that may not have been a gold-bearing region, the towns of Bath, Lyman, and Littleton had many small mines. The Dodge Mine in Lyman has produced $7,000 in gold. This was a very rich mine on the surface, but 100 feet down, the soil becomes slate, and there is no more gold to be found.

The wild Ammonoosuc River located in Landaff, just off Route 302, on the lower part of the river known as Big Boulder, has a lot of flower gold, which are good sized flakes, and occasionally a nugget can be found. This area is part of an ancient volcano mountain string, and the decomposing hillsides and flood plains seem to bring a lot of gold to the area.

Today, white Feldstar, white or rose quartz, flaky mica, and black tourmaline are mined in the White Mountains. Mica was formed when compressive forces in the earth's crust squeezed, distorted, and folded layers of mud. The heat caused by this effect had fused and completely transformed mud into the crystalline rock.

Franconia Notch

Franconia Notch was at one-time a rendezvous for thieves and outlaws. One of the caves in the area was known as a counterfeiters' den. It is said that a pack peddler with gold in his pockets was seen entering the trail one day. He was never seen again. It is as though he never came out of the Notch. The gold he was carrying is still said to be in the area. The peddler's body may still be in the mountains, but it is probable that the gold is not. Of course, he could have died by accident in a fall, cave-in, or landslide. If this is true, then the gold *could* still be where it was left.

Legends of Gold

Nathaniel Hawthorne once wrote a story based on an old legend of the area. The tale goes like this. There was once a man named Gathergold. He left the valley where he resided to seek his fortune, and returned when he found it. He built a palace of marble in the valley, where his old home once stood. It was said that there were rooms built of silver and gold and a bedchamber that glittered. There has never been any trace found of this house.

Another tale in this area happened less than two miles north of where the "Old Man in the Mountain" was once located. It is an overgrown ghost town, which was an active town in 1859. It was a copper mining town, but on one day in August 1859, every person and animal disappeared from the town.

The Native Americans have always believed that this area was cursed, because it was built on an ancient burial ground. The day of the disappearance came with great thunder, and the sky turned blood red. There is documentation that the ground shook and the sky did take on a copper hue. It is said that sixty-one miners were crushed in a mine cave-in. The town became choked in copper dust and everyone must have died. The problem is that no one was found dead in the town; all that the searchers found when they reached the area were empty houses. No trace or word from any of the townspeople was ever reported.

Mount Monadnock

The area around Mount Monadnock is called the Monadnock Range, and tradition of the area tells of a Native American lead mine that was worked with very primitive tools. A Native American was said to have given a crude map of the location to a Mr. Farwell. He, or his descendants, have never found the mine.

This mountain keeps its secrets well. Monadnock is an Algonquin word meaning "the unexcelled mountain or the surpassing mountain." There is, however, another definition for this word. The word may also be derived from the French word, "monnaie," which means, "money or silver," and the Abenaki word "aden" for mountain, and "ock" for "at the place of." So, the name may really means "the silver mountain place." In fact, there is an unusual mineral found only in this mountain area called Sillimanite. This mountain also is the source of a strange roar at times. A storm is preceded for several hours by a roaring of this mountain. This roar can be heard for ten to twelve miles. This phenomenon has also been heard in other mountain areas, where forests grow near the mountaintops.

Waterfall sites and treasure play a major role in the White Mountains, just like in Maine. Reverend Henry Dunster, who came to New England in 1640 from England, is said to have deposited a pot full of gold coins into a solid rock near the foot of the high falls on the right side of the Souhegan River. Exactly how he got the coins into a solid rock is not fully explained, but for many years that story has been taken as the truth. To search for this lost gold, Deacon Dakin decided to blow up a rock to get this money. There is said to be a great hole in the rock on the side of the falls, but no wealth was ever found. The hole in the rock was claimed to be seen by many residents.

Mother Worcester's Treasure Dream

Dreams were what told Mother Worcester where she could find a large quantity of wealth. Mother Worcester was a deeply religious and influential person among her neighbors. In 1852, she dreamt that gold could be found in the ledge on the farther bank of the Beebe River, at the base of a waterfall in Campton Hollow. She was convinced that this dream was true and spent all her savings, as well as some of her neighbors' savings, on digging a passage, fourteen feet high at the opening and forty feet long, into the rocky edge. No gold was ever found, though traces of lead were discovered. Today, the area is called "Mother Worcester's Cave."

1816 Legend

The year 1816 was called the starving year, or the year without a summer. Today, it is known that a huge volcanic eruption caused a cloud that blocked out the sun, which caused the Earth to cool a bit during that time. In New England, there was a killing frost every month of the year and people were moving out of the area to keep from starving.

The legend of this time is told of a Mrs. Hayes who lived in the Dover, New Hampshire area. She had a trunk full of silver dollars, but was worried about the bad company her son was keeping. She was afraid that she would be robbed, so she decided to bury her money. She remembers passing the old Hayes burying ground through the pole bars and she went deep into the woods. She wandered for a while, and finally in the triangle formed by three trees, she dug a hole and placed the trunk, then recovered the hole with dirt. Days later, she went back to find the burying place, and could never could find it again. So, the trunk may still lie somewhere in that area.

Bungy-Jar

The wind would seem to be the cause of numerous natural phenomena in the White Mountains. There is a place called Bungy-jar or the Bungy-bull-a-bellowing area. On Sugar Hill in New Hampshire, on a perfectly clear day, if the south wind blows through Kinsman Notch, it will sound like surf beating on a seashore that no one can see. The noise keeps increasing until a storm has blown in. It is a sure thing that fog will come through the Notch, too.

The strange name of the area comes from the early days. Life was hard in the mountains when the first settlers came. There were no roads or an easy way through the mountains, except the natural passages called *Notches*. When settlers came to Franconia and Easton, they came through Kinsman Notch, because it was a more direct way through, then through Profile Notch or Littleton. Some settlers only stayed a year, and then moved to the more fertile areas farther down the valley. The ones who stayed said of those who moved out that they just "bunged out," and soon the area was called Bungy Corner, and then became Bungy-jar.

Moodus Sounds of the Mountains

Remember the strange sounds that were heard on Mount Monadnock discussed earlier? The next natural noise phenomena heard in these mountains has a mystical gem attached to it. The noises actually have a name; they are called Moodus Sounds.

The Native Americans claimed to hear strange noises from the mountains on a clear day since the beginning of time. These noises were supposedly coming from their Great Spirit on top of Mount Washington. The Moodus Sound was heard in the vicinity of Mount Washington in March 1746, on a warm day with no clouds around. The people that heard the sound were "alarmed with a repeated noise," which they supposed was the firing of guns.

These sounds are heard on warm, clear days and are said to sound like distant cannon fire. John Josselyn, a seventeenth century English naturalist who wrote extensively about New England, believed that the White Mountains were hollow. He thought that the rain hitting the top of the mountains caused the sound he heard there.

Some of the noises that were thought to be Moodus Sounds could have been distant thunder or landslides, but no one event can explain all of them. Even today no one really knows exactly what causes the sounds. These sounds have been heard in many mountain regions of the world. They are called Moodus Sounds because the Native Americans who lived in the area between Saybrook and Middletown, Connecticut, first described them. They claimed that the sounds came from a mountain called, Machimoodus, or "place of noises." The Natives claimed that it was the home of Hohbamako, who was the chief of the evil spirits. When they were first asked about what the sounds were, they claimed that he was upset at the arrival of the Europeans to his land, and the sounds were his displeasure. That may have been more wishful thinking on the part of the Native Americans, possibly hoping this was a way to scare the Europeans out of the area. Today, the mountain is called Mount Tom.

The actual legend on Mount Tom states that the reason this noise occurs is because of two giant pearls that were growing inside the mountain. They needed to be taken out to stop the noises. Supposedly, these pearls grow and when they become too large, they cause earthquakes, thus the noises would start to occur.

Sometime before 1791, a British scientist, Dr. Steele or Dr. Steel—the name is spelled differently in the stories—found a cave in the Mount Tom area where the pearls were growing. He destroyed one of the largest pearls, which would stop the noise for the short term. However, he advised that the smaller one was growing quickly, and that the noises would start again.

On May 16, 1791, the noises started again. Explosions were heard, and residents felt at least two earthquakes. The legend states that a native of the area saw an old man, with a large pearl, climbing down the mountain the next day. Suddenly, the noises stopped in the mountain.

Another variation of the legend states that Dr. Steel dug up two pearls of great value near the Salmon River, calling them carbuncles. He destroyed them, saying that the noises would stop for a while, probably years. When the pearls would start to grow, the noises would start again.

As an interesting side note here, this is not the only time that a carbuncle is said to exist in the mountains. The problem is that the historical definition of a carbuncle, which comes from the Bible, says that it is a glittering red color, and when held against the sun, it resembles a burning coal. The story of the White Mountain carbuncle that is said to exist on Mount Washington will be explored later in this chapter.

Meanwhile, back to the strange sounds heard in the mountains. Another version of the Dr. Steel story is that he went to the White Mountains to take the Great Carbuncle off Mount Washington, and that it was a pure sapphire throne created by the God of the Mountain. The problem here is that the Great Carbuncle of the White Mountains is a brilliant red, not bright blue as a sapphire. Those colors are not easily confused.

Mount Tom is at the junction of the Moodus and Salmon Rivers. That area seems to be the center of the noise. Supposedly, the noises start in a cave in an area called Cave Hill. Seekers of the noise can walk about forty rods into the cave, and the light they are carrying will suddenly go out. That is their cue to turn around and leave. The Native Americans also had a legend that the deep rumbling sounds were whirlwinds trying to escape from the caves.

People that experience the Moodus noises say that it sounds like a stone or a large body falling underneath the ground directly under their feet. The object falls down a considerable distance in the depths below. The sounds have been studied all over the world, but exactly what they are still remains unknown. The sounds could be storms gathering in the distance, earth noises before an earthquake, or atmospheric disturbances—the answer just is not known.

Just as an interesting side note to the Moodus sounds and pearls, in 1854, a fisherman claimed to find pearls in the clams at Mink Pond. Later, this was proven false, but the pond is still known as Pearl Pond.

The Infamous Roger's Rangers

Roger's Rangers were a group of men that were half woodsmen and hunters and half militia. They were known all over the country for their bravery. Their leader, Major Robert Rogers, was a man who the Native Americans claimed to be under the protection of the Great Spirit of the Mountain or Manitou. The reason for this was because there was a landslide on the northern end of Lake George, and he escaped a Native American attack by snow shoeing down the slide to the lake on March 13, 1758. Of course, the Native Americans were scared of mountain slides, fearing that this was the wrath of the Great Spirit, but the Major had no such fears. All he wanted to do was escape death or capture by the attacking Native Americans.

This fact in no way detracts from his feat, but the Native Americans became a bit in awe with him. It gave him a great advantage at times during the conflict with the tribes in the area. What actually happened was that he was pursued to the edge of the cliff; he threw his pack down the slide, reversed his snowshoes and backtracked to the head of a ravine before anyone saw him. When the Native people saw his tracks, they believed that he threw himself over the cliff to avoid capture. When they finally saw the Major at the bottom of the cliff, they believed that the Great Spirit helped and refused to kill him.

Manitou was the God who gave the White Mountains to the Native American people. If Rogers was under his protection, then no harm would come to him, no matter what the Native Americans did. This is just the beginning of the famous treasure legend of Roger's Rangers and the White Mountains. It is truly a fascinating story.

The group set out from Moosilauke Mountain to attack, sack, and plunder the St. Francis tribe in Canada in the Fall of 1759. The beginning of the trip set an ominous tone to the rest of the adventure. One of Roger's Rangers, Robert Pomeroy, while climbing Moosilauke Mountain either looking for food or running away, is said to have collapsed from exhaustion and died on the summit from starvation. A body was found years later at the site.

This mountain seems to be a place where many strange accidents occur. In 1825, Daniel Welch climbed this mountain, and is said to have gotten lost and fell into the great gorge just south of the peak. Since then, hunters and trappers say that they hear cries for help in the dark glen and have seen a white form glide through the trees in the area. It could be either Pomeroy or Welch. Those are only two of the people that are known to have died here.

This mountain was also the location of the Prospect House or Summit Hotel. One American guest is said to have studied alchemy in Europe. The residents in the area started to suspect that he was using their pets for his experiments. Then, one day, a child disappeared. The alchemist was blamed, and a posse was organized to bring him to justice. The residents claim that the doctor was seen heading for the mountain peak, and they followed him, but could not catch him. There was a storm coming, so the residents left him on the mountain in the storm, and he is said to have been found dead near the hotel site. Now, strange steps are heard and a shadowy figure is seen in the area.

Now back to the St. Francis treasure story. The facts of the story are as follows. Governor Amherst sent the Rangers into the St. Lawrence region to destroy and plunder the Native American village of the St. Francis de Sales in October 1759. The Native Americans lived in the St. Lawrence region, southwest of Quebec, Canada. Around one hundred fifty to two hundred men, dressed in green buckskin, launched a night attack on the Native American village of St. Francis.

The Rangers were said to be the first Europeans to ever set foot in this area of Canada. It was not considered a pleasant experience by those who were living there. The Rangers sailed down to the northern end of Lake Champlain and walked the rest of the way, which took about twenty-one days. Their orders were simple, attack the village at 4:00 am and show no mercy. Over two hundred Native Americans were killed during the raid, but many did manage to escape. Many of the tribe were in a deep sleep because the day before they were celebrating the wedding of their chief's son. It is said that two of the Rangers, men named Farrington and Bradley, broke into the wedding party's home and killed everyone there, taking all the wedding gifts as their prize.

The Rangers are said to have ransacked the church in the village. Some of the tribe was hiding there, and after killing them all, they took a golden chalice, two heavy gold candlesticks, a cross, a silver church plate, and a large silver statue of the Madonna, which is said to have weighed ten pounds and was two and a half feet tall. This statue was cast from pure silver and resided in the Catholic chapel in the Abenaki Native American village, supposedly worth over one million dollars, perhaps more. The priest tried to save the holy relics, but the Rangers shot him and took the items anyway.

The Rangers retreated through lower Cohos, hoping to reach the Connecticut River, but the Native Americans who survived chased the men, with the help of the French army. The Rangers decided to split up into nine groups of nine people each. All would go a different way, hoping to confuse their pursuers. Each group would take some of the treasure that had been stolen, so perhaps some of it would make it out. They hoped they would all make it home, but it was not meant to be.

One of the Rangers who had part of the treasure did manage to live to get home to tell the whole tragic story. This is what he said happened. Sergeant Amos Parsons led his group of nine away from the rest of the Rangers. Each group was hoping to elude capture by the pursuing Native Americans, but the woods were dense and the Rangers really did not know the area well. They were also running, scared, had a heavy load, and that would make it difficult to find the best, fastest, and safest way out of the wilderness. A captured Native American woman was forced by Parsons to guide them to safety. The woman led them into the Israel River valley. The Israel River was named after Israel Glines, a noted hunter and trapper of the region in the eighteenth century. His brother, John, gave the river the name. The Native American name for the river was Singawack, which meant "the foaming stream of the White Rock."

Parsons, who was quickly becoming insane, so the story goes, supposedly beat the Native American guide often. The guide absolutely refused to find food for the men. She is said to have poisoned Parsons with the fang of a rattlesnake and ran off, leaving the men to their fate. Parsons, who was carrying the statue of the Madonna, became very ill. It was either thrown or rolled into the Israel River downstream from the town of Jefferson by Parsons. If this is true, because the statue was very heavy, it probably sank deep into the river bottom. Parsons either tried to get the statue and fell into the river, or he jumped into the river to rescue the statue. Whatever happened, he died in the river.

The men buried the rest of their loot in a cave nearby, and desperately tried to find the way out. All but one man of this group perished on the trek home. When the survivor was finally found wandering around, his knapsack was filled with human flesh. Supposedly, the remains of some of the Rangers were found at the head of Fifteen Miles Falls. Another version of the story is that a male Native American guide poisoned Parsons with a rattlesnake fang, when he was handing him a birch bark map of the area.

The handful of Roger's Rangers that survived did meet at the shore of Lake Memphrmagog. Rogers also survived and went alone in a raft to find help for his men. By the time everyone who survived arrived home, all the treasure had disappeared and the men were so haunted by what they had done, and what had happened to them, that they never went back to search for anything.

In 1816, the golden candlesticks were found in a swamp near Lake Memphremagog. The name is a Native American term that means "beautiful waters." No other part of the church treasure was ever discovered. It is said that $40,000 in gold and silver coins and the church plate could be found on the west bank of the Connecticut River, near Bloomfield on County 105 in Essex County.

Several years after the massacre, climbers are said to have found a barkless spot on a pine tree at the entrance to a wild ravine. The bare spot had partially obliterated characters carved with some crude tool. Rusty buttons, decayed cloth, copper kettles and some metallic parts of a gun were also found. There is also the story that a hunter in the area found a hatchet and birch bark covered with the wax from bees. Inside the wax, he found a fawn skin that was covered with mysterious hieroglyphics that were never deciphered. Perhaps they were about the lost treasure, or a map from one of the groups of Rogers Rangers.

There is more to this story. The mythical part of this legend states that the Native Americans placed a curse on the people who stole their treasure. The curse was placed by a dying member of the St. Francis tribe, probably the chief or Shaman. The curse is said to be,

"Great Spirit of the Abenaki will scatter darkness in the paths of the accursed English! Hunger walks before and death will strike their trails. Their wives weep for the warriors that do not return. Manitou is angry when the dead speak. The dead have spoken! He has spoken."

The reason the curse is said to have worked is because many of the Native American people killed were in the church or chapel where they were praying when the attack came. It was also said that the church bell kept ringing after the attack, but there was no one left to ring the bell. The fleeing Rangers said that they could hear the bell ringing for a long while, as they were retreating through the woods.

One night, years after the attack, a hunter is said to have been camping in the White Mountains. It was very foggy and the hunter heard organ music coming out of the darkness. He followed the noise, and the fog suddenly rolled back to reveal a great stone church. Inside there was an altar; from the middle was a sparkling curling wreath of intense smoke. All around it, lights dispersed a mellow glow, where the Native American people were kneeling in front of an altar, obviously praying in profound silence.

The scene suddenly changed, and a song was being sung, as a voice offering gifts to the Great Spirit was heard. The glittering church spire, church, and altar suddenly vanished and down the steep rock trail was a long line of strange looking men walking in silence. Before the line was a glittering silver image, which the men followed, disappearing into the rocks. There was then a loud harsh laugh, and nothing. Everything vanished right before the hunter's eyes. This part of the story should be taken with a grain of salt. Remember, the St. Francis tribe were killed in Canada, not the White Mountains. The treasure was lost here.

Another hunter was supposedly given a clue as to where and when the St. Francis treasure might be found. One night while in a deep sleep, he awoke when a voice cried out from all around him, "That pagan treasure from St. Francis may not remain a secret to adventure until the Great Spirit's thunder dies on the crags of Agiochook." Whatever that message meant is unclear, but the treasure has not been found yet.

As an interesting end to this very strange treasure story, Major Rogers of Rogers Rangers did survive the trek home, so perhaps the Great Spirit did really protect him. It is also claimed that he did not carry any of the St. Francis treasure with him. What is really interesting about this story is that part of it may be exaggerated. French observers of the raid stated, in an internal letter to their chain of command, that only thirty Native Americans were killed, and that twenty of them were women and children. Oral history of the St. Francis people say that a Mahican tribe member who was forced to be one of the Rangers scouts slipped into the village and warned them about the coming attack, so they could all leave.

Bigfoot Claims

To make this fascinating story complete, the first recorded sighting of the mysterious northern New England Bigfoot was in 1759, by members of Rogers Rangers. It is said that the members that survived the trek from the attack on the St. Francis tribe and were returning home and were just south of Missisquoi Bay in Vermont when something attacked them. One of the Rangers, a scout named Deluth, described the creature in his journal. He said that it looked like: "...a large black bear, who would throw large pine cones and nuts down upon us from trees and ledges..."

The Native Americans in the area called the monster Wejuk, meaning "wet skin" or "old slippery skin." To add more mystery and intrigue to this story, it should be noted that the men were close to Lake Champlain at the time, so perhaps there is more to the Lake Champlain lake monster story than we realize today. It should also be noted here that Champlain himself was told of this creature by the Abenaki people when he arrived at Missisquoi Bay. Whatever it was, it was said to have come out of the swamp there. Champlain never actually saw the creature; he just heard the tale. The New England Bigfoot monster story will be further explored in the Vermont Green Mountain chapter.

Great Carbuncle Mystery

Back to the White Mountains; there is another Native American legend about the Great Carbuncle, which is described as a blood red gem that is to be found on the highest mountain in the White Mountains. It is said to be suspended from a crag overlooking a dismal lake, called the Lake of the Clouds. This place would be Mount Washington.

The red carbuncle is said to be suspended from a dangerous ledge, which shines a dazzling red and golden luster at night. It lit the entire mountain top, and could be seen for miles. It is called the "great fire stone" and it is said that no mortal may ever touch it. If a human approaches the gem, which is guarded by the mountains, the wind will stir up the waters of the lake, causing a dark mist or fog to rise, which will cause the human to get lost.

The gem is guarded by an evil Native American spirit, who climbed the mountain and was killed on the spot to guard the treasure. If any mortal tries to search for it, they would be stricken with a peculiar madness forever. If, however, a mortal was lucky enough to touch this stone, it would become their talisman, and no danger could befall them on land or on sea. As the mortal approached the gem or got too close, the guardian would throw his fiery spear, hoping that the spear would either scare the seeker away or it would hit him to knock him off the cliff to a certain death.

The first European settlers claim to have seen this gem shining on the mountain. No matter how hard they tried to reach the stone, they never did see or find it as they neared the summit. No one really knows what was seen, but there were so many reports of a shining object that something must have been observed. That shining object is what caused the mountains to be called the crystal hills by the early explorers.

The Native Americans are said to have put a curse on the gem, they prayed that any seeker would not find the treasure because the Great Spirit would create a black storm of fire and thunder that would rend the cliff and bury the gem deeply in the ruins of rocks and trees. This curse for a landslide tends to lead to the thought that perhaps there was a great red gem, a garnet, possibly, that was buried in a landslide many years before the first Europeans came. This may be where the legends of the Great Carbuncle seen in the White Mountains were born. The landslide phenomena terrifies anyone who witnesses them, so it is not really surprising that these events would create a legend to help explain what was happening.

In the same area, after a horrible storm, a lost hunter claimed to see a skeleton from of a Native American suspended over a large chasm. As he approached, a red glare appeared from under the ledge. He left the area quickly to get help, but he could never find the exact spot again.

The Native Americans also claim that the stone just hung in mid-air, 2,000 feet above the head of a chasm at Oakes Gulf. The legend states that there is great wealth to be found on Mount Washington, and that a rocky ledge sends evil spells by crimson flashes down into the valley at night.

In 1642, Darby Field was the first European to ascend Mount Washington. It is believed that he went up to the ridge called Boott Spur, which is between Tuckerman's Ravine and the valley of the Dry or Mount Washington River. He brought crystals back, which he thought were diamonds. They were not, but could this be what the Native Americans and others saw, and why they believed a great gem existed nearby? Could a meteor sighting be the creator of this myth? For some unknown reason, meteors do not seem to fall in New England. There have been less than a dozen sightings since the Europeans first arrived here. The first documented meteor sighting in New England since the Europeans arrived was in Weston, Connecticut in the 1800s.

The Great Carbuncle also was said to be seen on Mount Monroe and is said to have been seen shining for miles around during the day and a dusky crimson at night. The early settlers in Saco, Maine, said that they saw a Great Carbuncle in the White Mountains, shining down on them, and it blinded them with its brilliance.

The Great Carbuncle is also said to be located in the glen of the Dry or Mount Washington River, which is a tributary of the Saco River, nearly opposite from the Frankenstein Cliff. It is said to be hidden under a shelving rock. No one can reach it, but it can be clearly seen. The Native Americans considered it a talisman against infection, who they considered to be the European settlers, and that it was overlooking the entire Saco River valley to protect them.

In fact, the entire Saco River area is considered a cursed place. The reason the river is cursed began in the summer of 1675. It is said that some obnoxious and drunk sailors from an English ship rowed up the Saco River, and saw a Native American woman who was paddling in a canoe with her baby son, named Menewee. The sailors decided that they would test the rumor that all Native American children could swim from birth. They attacked the woman and threw her baby into the raging river. The mother, who it is said was pregnant, jumped into the river to save her child. All three died. Her husband was a Native American chief called Squando, of the Sokokis tribe, and he was consumed with sadness and a great anger at those who had killed his family. He is said to have gone to the river and commanded it to take the lives of three people every year as revenge.

For many years, the river did as it was told. It was not until the mid-1940s that a year passed with no drownings. The Maine Sunday Telegram Newspaper headlined the event that year: "Saco River Outlives Curse of Indian Chief." Though many believe the curse is over, it is best to be cautious. Even in 2001, two people died on the Saco River, one man who drowned in Fryeburg and a boy who jumped off a bridge and broke his neck. On July 24, 2002, a young boy jumped off a bridge and was not found until the next day in ten feet of water. Whether it is ghosts or the curse, this area has many legends, and many have died in that dangerous raging river.

There are many Native American traditions about treasures of precious stones to be found in the mountains, especially gold and diamonds. Supposedly, others have seen these minerals, but only huge veins of granite and greenstone have been found. These stones are glinty and light colored, which may be the true reason why the mountains have been called the "Crystal Hills" at one time or another.

Perhaps there never was any great gem on top of the grand White Mountains. However, it can not be denied that something was seen on top of these places in earlier times. Perhaps the great carbuncle was destroyed, or hidden by nature or man, or perhaps it really is fire from the spirits who reside on that great mountain top.

Chapter Fourteen
Green Mountain
of Vermont Treasures

The New England mountains have always been places where the great spirits and the supreme being of the Native Americans lived. Though many feel that the New England tribes believed that the mountains were sacred for purely religious or supernatural reasons, the fact may actually be that there is a scientific reason for the Native American people to believe that there were magical beings living in the highest places. Perhaps it is true that the mountains really are enchanted and could bring death to those living in the valleys below.

The Abenaki, known as the "people of the dawnland," were the Native Americans that lived in New England for many years before the first ships appeared from the east and changed their lives forever. Though many of the first European settlers believed that Vermont was not populated, the western Abenaki families did dwell there, guarded by their creator, Odzihozo, who turned himself into a great rock, after creating all the valleys and hills of the region. When an western Abenaki family passed by the Guardian Rock, they always left an offering of tobacco to thank the creator for the land he had given them.

The Vermont Abenaki were more of a family group, than a community group. They followed the rhythm of the seasons and moved when they needed to. All the decisions made within the community were made by consensus, and the chiefs and leaders were followed by voluntary obedience. There was some contact with the rest of the Abenaki tribe members to the east, but it was a rare occurrence. This region was called Ndakinna, which meant, "our land." It was a very fluid and flexible civilization.

Abenaki Prophecy

The Abenaki told of an ancient prophecy that no one is exactly sure where it originated from. The prophecy foretold of a time, "when we must look for the coming of the man from the direction of the rising of the sun. This new era would bring a time of trouble for the Abenaki, knowing that a great change must follow his coming, it will make them weak and a weakness would overcome them, because the coming will put a bar to our happiness and our destiny will be at the mercy of events." The warning also told that, "when he comes, he will bring his children and women, he will come to stay, and he shall want all the land, because the land will be so sweet to him."

That prophecy is pretty amazing, since it was supposedly told many years before the Europeans actually came to New England. Though the Europeans did bring unknown disease to the Native Americans, without intending to, and Abenaki life changed forever, there was an earlier event that is said to have come from the sky, over the mountain that brought disease and death to the Abenaki. This death came from a carrier that shook the mountain when it arrived.

Vermont Comet Plague?

Comets, up until the seventeenth century, were considered bad omens when viewed. When Captain John Smith arrived in New England in 1619, he was told of a great plague that killed all the native people in the area, just one year earlier. There is no medical follow up from this report, just what the remaining Native Americans told Smith. The people told of seeing glowing lights in the sky, flying over the western mountains, and that disease came soon after. This plague effected both the east and west Abenaki, and since there was little contact between the two, some other link must exist to explain the mass death that occurred.

Many Abenaki who lived during that time came down with a putrid fever. The body took on a yellow sheen, much like yellow fever, but it is not thought that this was the cause. The disease spread very quickly through the entire New England region. It reduced the native population from ten thousand men to just a few hundred men in a very short period of time. As suddenly as it appeared, the disease disappeared, and left the survivors wondering what happened.

There was something unusual that happened worldwide through this period. Three comets were witnessed and documented as passing through Earth's atmosphere in 1618. The Chinese, Koreans, and Europeans all wrote of what was happening over the skies.

The year 1618 was the first year that comets were seen through telescopes. The first of these comets was witnessed in Hungry on August 25, where it rose in the morning sky with a blue-white tail pointing west. It was said to be difficult to see in the sun's glare.

The second comet was seen by observers in mid-November, also rising in the morning horizon. The head of the comet was below the horizon, but the tail was well above the horizon. The third comet was the most impressive and seen in early December. This comet was exiting from the solar glare with the tail projecting well above the horizon. The head laid beneath the horizon, but the tail reached impressive proportions above the horizon in mid-December. The comet was last seen on January 22, 1619. It is very possible that this was just one comet orbiting the sun and seen at different stages, but it is impossible to know for sure.

It is also documented that the entire world suffered from plagues after those comet sightings. Perhaps Earth did pass through the comet's tail, and that cause some strange cosmic virus to almost completely destroy the native population that lived in New England. Whatever happened, the native people believed that death came from above and feared the mountains even more.

It is not hard to wonder what may have happened if the plague of 1618 had not occurred. What if there were tens of thousands of Abenaki living in New England when the Europeans first arrived, instead of just hundreds? Would history have been different? Would the Abenaki prophecy had a different meaning? Perhaps this is one piece of evidence that confirms that what happens in space does, and can, effect Earth's history. Perhaps the dinosaurs would also agree, if they still existed.

Does it still seem difficult to believe that some celestial, or space, object caused something catastrophic to happen in New England? This would not be the first time, however. It has happened before. One of the easiest features to recognize from space in North America is the Manicouagan Crater, which lies right over the Vermont and Canadian border. This ancient asteroid crater is all that is left of an asteroid that smashed into this place about 212 million years ago. This impact may have been partly responsible for an extinction event within the Triassic period that wiped out up to eighty percent of the species living on the Earth at that time.

Green Mountain, One Name

Vermont is a mountain state, of that there is no doubt. That fact usually means two things, a smaller population settles there, and it is very difficult to travel around. Fewer people living in the area can mean that it is easier to hide things, and that precious ores can be mined easier in a mountain state, than in an ocean state.

The Green Mountain in Vermont is one complete range, not multiple ranges of mountains. Usually the mountain is called the Green Mountains, but that is incorrect. The mountain is located mainly in Vermont, which is the second largest New England state. Maine has the largest single stand alone mountain called Mount Katahdin. At this point, readers may be thinking, but Mount Washington in New Hampshire is the largest mountain in New England. Mount Washington is the highest peak in the Presidential Range of the White Mountains, not a single mountain. The name Vermont is said to be for this mountain range. The name comes from the French words, "Verd" and "Mont," which means Green Mountain.

The mountain is an elongated mountain and very few of the peaks are barren, which is why the mountain appears to be green. The green color also comes from the rock the mountain is made from, chlorite. This is the northern link of the Appalachian chain. Like the White Mountains, the vegetation that lives on this mountain likes limestone rock. Though the state is not near the ocean today, in 1849, the skeleton of a marine whale was found in Charolette, Vermont, which seems to prove that at least in ancient times, Vermont must have been near or under salt water.

The Green Mountain was formed at the close of the Paleozoic Era. This was the great mountain building period, known as the Appalachian Revolution. At this time, the Green Mountain area was raised into a lofty mountain range and produced intense crushing and metamorphism of the rocks. This was happening all through the Appalachian chain. The Green Mountain was completely formed 440 million years ago. This is the oldest mountain in New England. The high and dry passes through the mountain were created by the wind, and the low and wet passes through the mountain were created by water. The mountain has many different types of stones that were created by the intense pressure of its birth beneath its surface.

The southern crest of the mountain has the oldest rocks known in New England, dating from the Pre-Cambrian age, residing there called Gneiss. Gneiss is a metamorphic successor to the igneous granite of the area. It is distinguished from granite by its unique type of bending or stratification that it exhibits, which creates many intricate folds that look like a coarse grained granite.

There is also a metamorphic rock that is almost pure quartz found here. It was originally sandstone, but the metamorphic rock is now called quartzite. This rock looks like maple sugar. Its freshly broken surface will glisten in the sun. It is hard to break, even harder than granite, and a hammer stroke will make sparks and often create a peculiar odor.

Mountain Road Treasure

In earlier times, there was only one public route across the Green Mountain called the Crown Point Highway. It was not much of a highway, at that. The width was three rods, which all roads had to be, but anything could and did lie between the borders of those rods. That included boulders, stumps, swamps, forests, as well as a mountain. It would be, and was, the perfect place to hide valuables, either one's own or ones that were taken. That is exactly what happened here. In 1952, Tom Penfield found two treasures that were buried by the Spanish on Ludlow Mountain, a peak of the Green Mountain. One of the treasures was gold.

Lake Champlain

In 1787, the first settlers of the upper Lake Champlain area were Hessian troops. They actually believed that they were settling in Canada, not Vermont. There is a story that there is a buried treasure on Stave Island, just north of Mallet's Bay in Lake Champlain hidden by these troops.

Smuggler Treasure

Vermont and Canada had border controversies in the 1800s. In Highgate Springs, smugglers actually fought with the revenue agents during this time. St. Albans is the shire town of Franklin County, and between 1807 and the War of 1812, it was the largest base of smuggling on Lake Champlain. President Jefferson had put an embargo on England and that put a major strain on the people of Vermont who were trading with Canada. The people of Vermont considered the embargo unfair, so they decided to ignore it and smuggle goods to Canada. The best way to do this was through and over the wild Vermont mountain. The famous smuggling ship, *Black Snake*, which was finally captured, smuggled thousands of dollars worth of merchandise to Canada and back. Perhaps hiding loot all along the way.

Civil War and Vermont

The people of New England tend to think of the Civil War as something that they participated in, but it was really fought in the southern part of the country. This is not exactly true. On October 19, 1864, the most northerly engagement of the Civil War took place. It is called the Day of the St. Albans Raid. At 3:00 pm, twenty-two Confederate soldiers stole $114,522 from three St. Albans banks in gold coins and paper currency. The legends states that the soldiers were pursued and buried the loot in the vicinity of Highgate Springs, just off U.S. 89, near Lake Champlain in the northwestern corner of the state in Franklin County.

The leaders of the raid were eventually caught and had a trial in Canada, but were freed because the raid was considered an act of legitimate warfare. There was so much international ill will caused by this act, that the Canadian Parliament gave $50,000 in gold to Vermont to help defray the financial loss. The actual loot was never found.

Smugglers Notch

Smugglers Notch was created by liquid water, cut as the glacial water that poured from the Champlain Valley into the Stowe Valley. The Notch was never open in the winter; it was way too narrow and steep to plow. The name comes from the massive smuggling of cows from the area to Canada in the 1800s. The smugglers would get the cattle safely to a ford at the Lamoille River, where they could get safely to Canada.

The Notch was also used extensively during the prohibition era. Smuggled bootleg flowed through the Notch down to central and southern New England. It is possible that there may be caches or hidden stores of the alcohol in the caves all around the Notch. The caves were the perfect temperature for storing the hidden loot.

Though farm animals were the major source of smuggling through the Notch, there have been stories about several treasures caches buried about ten miles east of the area. This is a rugged pass, so it is not surprising that authorities had such a hard time stopping the smuggling there. There are caves in the area and the rocks still tumble to the floor at the Notch, today. It is said that it would take a dozen semi-trucks to haul the treasure that is buried just south of Jefferson and Cambridge. There is no doubt that this notch is very special. Just to make sure that everyone realizes how special this place is, there are plants that grow there today, that grow no where else in Vermont.

Province Island Loot

Province Island on Lake Memphremagog supposedly hides a treasure that was buried by a smuggler called Skinner. He hid it there to avoid the law, but is said to have never went back for it. This is the same lake that Roger's Rangers were to meet, if they survived the trek through the White Mountains. If any of the St. Francis treasure was still with any of the Rangers, it may also be buried here.

Mining Craze

There has been silver and gold mined in Vermont. Early in the nineteenth century, a sixty-eight dollar lump or nugget of gold was discovered in Somerset in the Deerfield River. Additionally, there was a half-pound nugget of gold found in Newfane in Windham County. Both of these finds caused a gold rush of sorts to the area to mine for the yellow ore. Also in Windham County, gold has been found in the south branch of the Rock River near Dover and in the south branch of the Saxton's River near Grafton. Turkey Mountain has been a place where gold has been found, as well. Gold has also been said to have been found in Whetstone Brook near Jamaica, Adams Brook near Marlboro, and the West Brook near Townsend.

Mining really did not begin until 1851, when the first vein of gold was discovered in Bridgewater in Windsor County. There were mines in this area and gold was found in the Williams River, Trout Brook, Locust Creek, Broad Brook, Dimick Brook, Gold Brook, Black River, Jewell Brook, Buffalo Brook, Hall Brook, Hollow Brook, and Piney Hollow Brook. The big Green Mountain gold mining discovery occurred in Calvin Coolidge County near Plymouth and Tyson. One nugget pulled from the area was worth seventeen dollars. In 1880, the Plymouth Gold Mine Company came to town with $50,000 to invest in finding whatever gold there was in the Five Corners area.

When one company moves in, then others will be sure to follow. The Rooks Mining Company moved into the area and word leaked out that a valuable deposit of ore had been found. A long tunnel was dug into the mountain and gold bars suddenly started appearing in town. Mr. H. L. White, treasurer of the Rooks Mining Company, exhibited a gold bar worth $2,081, which was said to have been made from ore found in the cave. This was enough to create an interest in investing in the company, but in the end, there was not enough gold to even pay back all the investors. It even appears that the bar was not really made from Vermont gold at all.

Though there was gold found here, it was not a rich strike like those of the west. People were able to make rings, watches, or necklaces out of what they found, but not much more. The author believes that the Vermont state geologist of 1904 said it best, "There is gold in Vermont, but widely distributed and in so small quantities that the cost of collecting it is far greater than the value of the gold obtained."

There are said to be two lost Native American mines in Vermont. One is a silver mine and the other is a gold mine, though it is hard to believe that there actually could have been a gold mine in Vermont. Somewhere on Mount Mansfield in the southwest corner of Lamoille County is said to exist the Lost Slayton Gold Mine.

Mount Mansfield

Mount Mansfield rises 4,393 feet in elevation and one of the few peaks of this mountain that is bare on top. The mountain is three miles long and is really a group of peaks that are connected by a succession of summits, which are connected by a ridge. The outline of the mountain is of an upturned face. The Native Americans called this mountain, Moxe-o-de-be-wadso, which means "mountain with a head of a moose."

There is also a Native American legend about why this mountain looks the way it does. A son of a chief, in order to be worthy of becoming a chief, had to prove himself to his tribe. Despite the fact that he had crippling disabilities, he climbed to the summit, only to be killed in a raging storm. After the clouds disappeared, the mountain took on his features, staring up at the sky.

One of the more interesting objects on this mountain is a boulder that sits on one of the summits. It is a specimen of rock called labradorite. The nearest bed of this type of rock is 125 miles away, northwest of Quebec. This piece was left here when the glacier receded. As an interesting side note, this area is also the home of the weird creatures called Woods Walkers. This legend takes on Bigfoot legend qualities. It is considered a good idea to avoid these creatures whenever possible. It is not considered a good omen to see them or to even have contact with them.

Lost Mine and Golden Rivers

Somewhere between Sherbourne Pass, which is 2,190 feet high and Pico Peak, and located about fifteen miles northeast of Rutland in Rutland County, there is said to be a lost mine called the Lost Birch Hill Silver Mine. Pico Peak is considered one of Vermont's highest peaks, rising to 3,967 feet. It is one of the peaks that encircle Killington.

There have been eight different rivers in this area that have claims of gold being discovered. Gold Brook, Little River and the west branch of the Waterbury River near Waterbury have all produced gold. The Rattling Brook near Belvidere, the first branch of the Lamoille River near Cambridge, the Gibon River and North Branch River near Johnson, and the Sterling Brook near Morristown, are places where seekers have found gold at one time or another.

Bennington Monster

In the Glastenbury Mountain area, it is said that strange lights, untraceable sounds, and spirits have been seen since pre-colonial times. Native Americans never came to this area; they believed that it was cursed. All they would do here was bury their dead. So, this place is a Native American burial site.

In the nineteenth century, a coach full of people were said to be attacked by the "Bennington Monster," which has characteristics of the western Bigfoot legends. There is no doubt that something walks in the Vermont woods that no one has been able to explain. Perhaps it is a guardian of the lost mines and treasure that is said to exist there?

Bennington Treasure Story

There is also a treasure story about the Bennington area. The British, at various times in the state's history, seemed to hide many treasures within Vermont's boundaries. It does make some sense as to why they did hide their treasure here. It was very difficult to move through the state, and its land is connected to Canada. At Harmon Hill, which is located about five miles southeast of Bennington, the British buried several kegs of silver coins, after being defeated at the Battle of Sarasota and retreating through this area.

The Bennington Battle Monument is located west of Bennington on State 7. Patriot raiders robbed $90,000 in silver and gold coins from a British supply train, and supposedly buried the coins in this area before they were caught and shot—without telling anyone where they had hid their loot.

Remember the St. Francis treasure and Rogers Rangers from the previous chapter? There have been reports of some of the Rangers getting really lost, and ending up on the west bank of the Connecticut River near Bloomfield in Essex County. It is here that some of that treasure may have been buried.

This may be more of a hidden treasure area than one would think. At Fort Drummer, which is located three miles southeast of Brattleboro on the Connecticut River in Windham County, there have been five small caches of Revolutionary War period silver and gold coins found.

This region was first settled in 1773. In 1775, most of the settlers left to fight with Ethan Allen in the Revolutionary War. It is thought that many of the early settlers buried their treasure around their old homesteads. They believed that they might never return home. Unfortunately, many of them did not return, and their buried treasure could remain on their old homesteads.

Marble-Rich

There are abandoned marble quarries in this region. On Mount Aeolus, there is a quarry of marble deposits. There are heaps of marble fragments that were discarded by the miners lying around here with grass growing on top of them. Mount Aeolus is named for the God of the Winds, because in 1860, some students from Amherst College were on top of the mountain when a strong wind was blowing. They christened the mountain with the name Aeolus by pouring a bottle of water over its rocks. The dark side to the story is that, in some versions, one of the students fell over the cliff, being pushed by the strong wind and died from the fall.

Mount Ascutney is the place where a rare type of marble was found. It is called dark syenite, which is what is used to build the magnificent columns at the library of Columbia University.

Rutland is the shire town of Rutland County. It is called the "marble city" and for a good reason. The marble deposits discovered on the west side of town are among the richest in the world.

There is a valley, called the Otter Creek Valley, in West Rutland, Vermont, in the Proctor area that was once the home of the Vermont Marble Company. The family that owned the company was the Proctors. This was the richest and most productive marble deposit ever found in the United States. The marble from this area was used to build the United Nations Building in New York, the Supreme Court Building in Washington, D. C., and for Roosevelt's Tomb at Hyde Park. The Taconics Mountains on the west and the Green Mountain on the east created this marble-rich valley.

Camel's Hump

The most striking feature of the area is Camel's Hump. This is a bare rock cone, which means it's bare on top, and to the French soldier that supposedly gave its name, it looked like a crouching lion. He was sailing on Lake Champlain and when he looked to the east and saw the peak, he cried "Le Lion Couchant," which is French for the crouching lion. It is thought that the soldier meant that the lion appeared to be resting. Actually, the crouching lion is a lion that is ready to attack.

In 1798, it was called Camel's Rump, but was changed, in 1824, to Camel's Hump. The Native Americans, who lived in the area, called it Tawabodewadso, which meant "the mountain that is like a seat" or the "resting place mountain." The peak rises 4,099 feet above the sea with trees covering the southern part, while the northern part is covered in bare rock. There are three mysterious and hidden treasure legends about this peak.

In July 1609, Samuel de Champlain wrote about this peak, "it is a very high peak capped with snow." The mystery is why did he write that this mountain was covered with snow in July? What did he really see? Is it possible to have snow on the mountain in July? No one really knows for sure, but usually this peak does not have snow cover in July. It has never occurred since.

The next story is that on October 16, 1944, a B-24 bomber plane from Westover Air Force Base crashed there. It was a very cold, moonless night, and the first snowfall topped the peak. The plane was traveling at 215 miles per hour at 4,000 feet when the plane slammed into the mountain. It cart-wheeled toward the south, ripping off its tail section and landing against a tree. The forward section was completely disintegrated. Nine members of the crew died instantly. James Wilson was the only survivor. He endured two nights on this peak before being rescued. He lost both hands and his feet to frostbite. Today, there is virtually no trace of the crash site. Climbers state that there is an unexplained, strange silence around this site.

The third story is that in the late 1700s, a rich silver vein was found there. The story goes that the miners who found the silver had to leave the United States rather quickly, though why they had to leave is not revealed. They decided to leave the silver behind, so when they returned, they could retrieve it. They buried the smelted silver in the mouth of a cave, where Lake Champlain could be seen clearly. The entrance to the cave is located on the east side of the lake. Though searches have been made, no silver or silver vein has ever been found.

There was a very rich copper vein found in the piedmont of the mountain. Piedmont means "at the foot of the mountain." The eastern foot of the Green Mountain hides a belt of schist type of rock, and extends from the Canadian border south to Bellows Falls, Vermont. This belt no longer produces copper, but in its heyday, this one area produced forty percent of all the copper used in the United States.

Addison County Loot

Addison County has a rich lore of treasure and ghosts. Gold has been found in the Baldwin and Lewis Creek near Bristol. The most famous treasure story about this area is found in Hell's Half Acre, located in Bristol, Vermont, about two miles south of town on an old country back road. This town was called Pocock at the time when the treasure said to be buried here was hidden. The area is rich in treasure history and it is also said that the British could have buried $200,000 in the area.

It is a strange place. Geologists call this ridge a Hogback Anticline. The western edge of the Green Mountain is a very rocky place, and the Bristol Cliffs, also called the Talus Field, is created by a ragged rectangle of pale gray Cheshire Quartzite that is constantly renewed as more huge blocks of stone tumble down the steep cliff. This process turns over the un-lichened side of the stones, and they glint in the sun. The Cheshire formation began as sand that was deposited on an ocean shelf, 600 million years ago. This was before the plate collision that created the Appalachians occurred. The sand was metamorphosed into quartzite and lifted onto the mountain by the great pressure of re-converging plates 445 million years ago.

There are unique natural features here, as well as man-made features that mark this place as eerie. There is a jagged rock on top of the Bristol Cliffs called the Devil's Pulpit. There is the Notch in the mountain where the loggers shot the logs through in the winter called the Devil's Cart Road. The Talus slope is also called Rattlesnake Den. The people, who came to look for lost treasure, would also hunt for rattlesnakes on a Sunday afternoon.

It is considered an enchanted, as well as mysterious, place. The spirits that dwell here are to be have been sacrificed to guard the treasure that is buried here. There are tales by treasure hunters of a dog that was killed here, as well as a ghost boy, who has been seen with a gash across his neck. These supernatural spirits must be guarding the treasure very well, because nothing has been found here yet.

There are actually two treasure stories about this unique area. One is about the British fleeing the Patriots and their treasure. The other is about a Spanish or French miner called DeGrau.

Revolutionary War Era Treasure

A treasure said to consist of seventy-five pounds of British gold was buried by British Officers, who were fleeing the Patriots during the Revolutionary War era. It is also said that they buried silver coins on the southern shores of Lake Mephremagog, near Newport on State 5. This lake is the northern boundary between the United States and Canada.

It is thought that perhaps the British found some of the old Spanish treasure and took it, but buried it while fleeing to another place, or it is the same as the Bennington treasure story, but the places are mixed up. Anyway, the loot is still called the Hell's Half Acre Treasure.

Legends of the entire Green Mountain area tell that Spanish miners had unearthed pounds of silver ore, but they mined so much, that they could not get it out of to the ocean where the Spanish treasure ship was waiting. This was a very wild and remote place in the early days. The Spanish, or French, depending on the version of the story, were said to leave much of their gold and silver behind. The old Spanish or French buried treasure is buried somewhere in the caves of the White Rocks Mountain in Wallingford. There are stacks of silver coins and tons of bullion just left by fleeing Spanish or French miners. These piles are apparently waiting for the miners to return to retrieve them or for some other treasure seeker to find. So far, no one has found the missing gold or silver. No one is sure exactly why the Spanish or French were fleeing, either, especially without the loot or a map of the area to find the treasure. This story sounds a lot like the story of Camel's Hump. It is perhaps a case of mistaken identity.

Bristol Money Diggings

The second story of this treasure is called the Bristol Money Diggings, which took place on the Talus slopes. The legend goes on to say that in 1801, some boys saw an old man digging on the south end of the slope. No one knew him, so the boys went over, and the man growled at them and menaced them with a shovel. The boys went home and told their father who immediately went out to see who was there.

The man told them that he was the son of a man named DeGrau, a Spanish miner, who said that he buried a great amount of silver or had hidden a silver mine, on a ledge near the Talus slope area. The son was looking for this mine, but was having a hard time finding it. Many people in the town turned out to help him, but no silver was ever found.

It may be that the two prior stories are related. There may be silver buried, but the seekers could be searching in the wrong place. Here are more facts of the confusing case. There is said to be a lost silver mine somewhere near Wallingford. The legend states that the Spanish was smelting the silver taken from the silver vein just outside the mouth of the mine. (Smelting is when the miner pours the liquid silver into molds to form ingots, then would store the molds into caves.) Some of the crew went in search of food and supposedly got lost. Eventually, they made it back to a ship. It is said that while this crew was lost they wandered into southern Vermont, and while looking for shelter in a low mountain range, they discovered an outcrop of silver. Perhaps it was the mother lode that they were working on in another part of the state. Deciding to mine the silver after finding their ship, they could not ever find the silver vein again.

Possibly only one Spanish crewmember ever returned to the area and was found digging by a local boy, Richard Lawrence. Perhaps the miner told this story to the boy for helping him, after the miner had broken his own arm. He gave the boy directions to the silver vein, but before Lawrence could retrieve the silver, a landslide occurred completely covering the entrance to the ore.

The other name that is associated with this story is Phillip DeGrau, who was supposedly a crewmember of the ship, *Nebuchadnezzar*. His story is that members of the crew took eight heavy chests from the ship, filled them with treasure from the old Spanish mine, but could only take four chests with them. They left the other four chests to be picked up at another time. That time never came. Phillip said that, on a western-facing slope of the Green Mountain, the chests were buried in the floor of a shallow cave in the exposed rock face of a low peak. The sailors closed off the entrance with rocks and forest debris. The next day, they saw the town of Pocock, which is Bristol today. They never found the treasure again.

To add even more confusion to this story, another version states that in 1752, four Spanish deserters from the galleon, called the *San Jose*, took 80,000 gold doubloons from the ship's treasure stores. Native Americans attacked them, while they were burying the gold. Since their horses were killed during the attack, they had to walk out of the wilderness, but could not find their way back. The gold was buried in a space between two giant rocks in the area.

So it would seem that there is a lost silver mine with numerous silver ingots stored inside, still to be found, as well as a virgin silver vein. There may be gold and silver bars that are buried here that were taken from treasure ships, or even treasure taken from the silver mine, and buried here in a cave that has been hidden by a landslide, or perhaps an earthquake. Landslides do happen in these mountains quite often, and as has been seen in previous chapters, the word can conjure fear in anyone. Rock, snow, mud, and water slides all play a part in creating and destroying these mighty mountains, and whatever still may be hidden in them.

It is interesting to note that on November 18, 1706, there was a large earthquake in this area. Perhaps something is buried under the earth. It appears that perhaps green is not the only color that can be found in Vermont, if the treasure seeker looks hard enough.

Conclusion

So, our quest for ghostly treasure comes to an end. Or does it? There are many unknown treasures that still may exist somewhere in northern New England. It just takes patience, research, luck, and no fear of what may still be guarding the treasures said to remain in New England.

Bibliography

Anderson, John & Sterns, Morse. *Book of the White Mountains*. New York, New York: Minton, Balch, & Co., 1930

Attwood, Stanley Bearce. *The Length and Breadth of Maine*. Augusta, Maine: Kennebec Journal Print Shop, 1946

Bachelder, Peter Dow. *Lighthouses of Casco Bay*. Cape Elizabeth, Maine: Provincial Press, 1995

Bartlett, Stanley Foss. *Beyond the Sowdyhunk*. Falmouth, Maine: Falmouth Book House, 1937

Bearse, Ray. *Vermont: A Guide to the Green Mountain State*. Boston, Massachusetts: Houghton Mifflin Co., 1966

Beck, Horace P. *Gluskap the Liar and other Indian Tales*. Freeport, Maine: The Bond Wheelwright Co., 1966

Beck, Horace P. *The Folklore of Maine*. Philadelphia, Pennsylvania: J. B. Lippincott, Co.,1957

Blakemore, Jean. *Treasure Hunting in Maine*. Boothbay Harbor, Maine: The Smiling Cow Shop, 1952

Botkin, B.A. *A Treasury of New England Folklore Stories, Ballads & Traditions of the Yankee People.* New York, New York: Crown Publishers, 1947

Botting, Douglas. *The Seafarers: The Pirates.* Alexandria, Virginia: Time Life Books, 1978

Bowers Q. David. *American Coin Treasures and Hoards.* Irvine, California: Bowers & Merena Galleries, 1997

Cahill, Robert, Ellis. *Haunted Happenings.* Danvers, Massachusetts: Old Saltbox Publishing, 1992

Cahill, Robert Ellis. *Lighthouse Mysteries of the North Atlantic.* Salem, Massachusetts: Old Saltbox, 1998

Cahill, Robert Ellis. *New England's Mountain Madness.* Danvers, Massachusetts: Old Saltbox Publishing, 1989

Cawthorne, Nigel. *A History of Pirates: Blood and Thunder of the High Seas.* Secaucus, New Jersey: Chartwell Books, 2004

Citro, Joseph A. *Green Mountains, Dark Tales.* Hanover, New Hampshire: University Press of New England, 1998

Clair, Colin. *Unnatural History.* London, England: Abeland-Schman, 1967

Coffman, F.L. *1001 Lost, Buried, or Sunken Treasures: Facts for the Treasure Hunters.* New York, New York: Thomas Nelson & Sons, 1957

Colesworthy, D.C. *Chronicles of Casco Bay*. Portland, Maine: Sanborn & Carter, 1850

Collins, Robert S. *Wescustogo & Aucocisco: True Tales of Maine Coast People Since 1636*. South Portland, Maine: Pilot Press, 1975

Cordingly, Donald. *Under the Black Flag*. New York, New York: Random House, 1995

Costopoulos, Nina. *Lighthouse Ghosts & Legends*. Birmingham, Alabama: Crane Hill Publishers, 2003

Crawford, Lucy. *Lucy Crawford's History of the White Mountains*. Hanover, New Hampshire: Dartmouth Publishers, 1845

Crooker, William S. *Tracking Treasure – In Search of East Coast Bounty*. Halifax, Nova Scotia: Nimbus Publishing, 1998

Dann, Kevin. *Lewis Creek Lost and Found*. London, England: University Press of New England, 2001

Dietz, Lew. *The Allagash*. New York, New York: Holt, Rinehart & Winston, 1968

Dobie, J. Frank. *On the Open Range*. Dallas, Texas: Banks Upshaw and Co., 1931

Dow, George Francis. *The Pirates of the New England Coast 1630-1730*. Salem, Massachusetts: Marine Research Society, 1923

Drago, Harry Sinclair. *Lost Bonanzas*. New York, New York: Dodd, Mead & Co., 1966

Drake, Samuel Adams. *Heart of the White Mountains: Their Legend and Scenery*. Franklin Square, New York: Harper & Brothers Publishing, 1882

Eckstorm, Frannie Hardy. *John Neptune & Other Maine Indian Shamans*. Portland, Maine: The Southworth-Anthoensen Press, 1945

Early, Eleanor. *Behold the White Mountains*. New York, New York: Little, Brown, & Co., 1935

Elder, John. *Reading the Mountains of Home*. Cambridge, Massachusetts: Harvard University Press, 1998

English, J. S. *Indian Legends of the White Mountains*. Boston, Massachusetts: Rand Avery Supply Co., 1915

Ford, Barbara & Switzer, David C. *The Excavation of a revolutionary war privateer: Under Water Dig*. New York, New York: William Morrow & Co., 1982

Freucher, Peter with Loth, David. *Peter Freucher's Book of the Seven Seas*. New York, New York: Simon & Schuster, 1957

Gudde, Erwin G. *1000 California Place Names*. Los Angeles, California: University of California Press, 1969

Haydock, Tim. *Treasure Trove, where to find the great lost treasures of the world*. New York, New York: Henry Holt & Co., 1986

Haynes, William. *Casco Bay Yarns*. New York, New York: D. O. Haynes & Co., 1916

Hitching, Francis. *The Mysterious World: An Atlas of the Unexplained*. New York, New York: Holt, Rinehart, & Winston, 1978

Jameson, W. C. *Buried Treasures of New England*. Little Rock, Arkansas: August House Publishers, 1998

Jerome, John. *On Mountains, Thinking about Terrain*. New York, NY: McGraw-Hill Book Co., 1978

Jones, Herbert G. *King's Highway from Portland to Kittery*. Portland, Maine: The Longfellow Press, 1953

Jones, Herbert Granville. *The Isles of Casco Bay in Fact & Fancy*. Freeport, Maine: Bond Wheelwright, 1946

Johnson, Merle. *Howard Pyle's Book of Pirates:Fiction, Fact & Fancy concerning the Buccaneers & Marooners of the Spanish Main, Writings and Pictures of Howard Pyle*. Franklin Square, New York: Harper & Brothers Publishing, 1921

Kennedy, B.F., Jr. *Buried Treasure of Casco Bay*. New York, New York: Vantage Press, 1963

Kilbourne, Frederick, W. *Chronicles of the White Mountains*. Boston, Massachusetts: Houghton Mifflin Co., 1916

Kunz, George Frederick. *The Curious Lore of Precious Stones*. Philadelphia, Pennsylvania: J.B. Lippincott Co., 1913

Ladd, Richard S. *Map: Explorers routes, trails and early roads in U.S.* Library of Congress Catalog card

Lee, W. Storrs. *The Green Mountain of Vermont*. New York, New York: Henry Holt & Co., 1955

Leland, Charles G. *The Algonquin Legends of New England*. Boston, Massachusetts: Houghton, Mifflin & Co., 1884

Manley, David F. *Pirates and Privateers of the Americas*. Oxford, United Kingdom: ABC-CLIO, 1994

Marx, Robert & Jenifer. *New World Shipwrecks: 1492-1825*. Dallas, Texas: Ram Publishing Co., 1994

Marx, Robert. *Buried Treasures you can find*. Dallas, Texas: Ram Publishing, Co., 1996

McLane, Charles B. *Islands of the Mid-Maine Coast*. Rockland, Maine: Tibury House, Gardiner, Maine & Island Institute, 1992

McLouglin, William G. *Rhode Island: A Bicentennial History.* New York, New York: W.W. Norton & Co., 1978

Merrill, Daphne Winslow. *The Lakes of Maine: A compilation of Fact & Legend.* Rockland, Maine: Courier-Gazette, Inc., 1973

Mitchell, David. *Pirates.* New York, New York: The Dial Press, 1976

Mitchell, Edwin Valentine. *It's an Old State of Maine Custom.* New York, New York: The Vanguard Press, 1949

Moore, Robin & Jennings, Howard. *The Treasure Hunter.* Upper Saddleback River, New Jersey: Prentice-Hall, Inc., 1974

Morrill, Philip and a lot of other people. *Maine's Mines & Minerals – western Maine volume 1.* Naples, Maine: Dillingham Natural History, 1958

Morrill, Philip & Hinckley, William, P. *Maine's Mines & Minerals – eastern Maine volume 2.* Naples, Maine: Dillingham Natural History, 1959

Moulton, John K. *An Informal History of Four Islands, Cushing, House, Little Diamond, and Great Diamond.* Yarmouth, Maine: John. K. Moulton, 1991

Munson, Gorham. *Penobscot – Downeast Paradise.* Philadelphia, Pennsylvania: J. B. Lippincott Co., 1959

Nutting, Wallace. *New Hampshire Beautiful*. Garden City, New York: Garden City Publishing, 1937

Nutting, Wallace. *Vermont Beautiful*. Garden City, New York: Garden City Publishing, 1936

Otis, James. *An Island Refuge, Casco Bay in 1676*. Boston, Massachusetts: Estes & Co., 1895

Olzendam, Roderic M. *The Lure of Vermont's Silent Places*. Essex Junction, Vermont: Issued by: the Vermont Bureau of Policy, Vermont Office of Secretary of State, 1918

Pearl, Richard, M. *American Gem Trails*. New York, New York: McGraw-Hill Book Co.,1964

Peate, Roderick. *The Friendly Mountains*. New York, New York: The Vanguard Press, 1942

Perham, Jane C. *Maine Geographic: Gems & Minerals*. Freeport, Maine: Delorme Publishing Co., 1983

Pickford, Nigel. *The Atlas of Ship Wrecks and Treasure*. London, England: Dorling Kinderslery, 1994

Poole, Ernest. *The Great White Hills of New Hampshire*. New York, New York: Doubleday & Co., 1946

Quake, Walter Collins. *Trails & Summits of the Green Mountain*. Cambridge, Massachusetts: Houghton Mifflin Co., & Riverdale Press, 1926

Randall, Peter E. *Mount Washington: A Guide and Short History.* Woodstock, Vermont: The Countryman Press, 1983

Rankin, Hugh F. *The Golden Age of Piracy.* New York, New York: Holt, Rinehart & Winston, Inc., 1873

Raymo, Chet & Raymo, Maureen C. *Written in Stone.* Guilford, Connecticut: The Globe Pequot Press, 1989

Rich, Louise Dickinson. *The Coast of Maine: An informal History.* New York, New York: Thomas Y. Cromwell Co., 1956

Room, Adrian. *Place Names of the World.* Lanham, Maryland: Rowman & Littlefield, 1974

Rutledge, Lyman V. *The Isles of Shoals in Lore and Legend.* Barre, Massachusetts: Barre Publishing, 1965

Schwartz, Alan. *Gold and Sliver – Silver and Gold: Tales of Hidden Treasure.* New York, New York: Harper Collins, 1983

Schlosser, S.E. *Spooky New England.* Guilford, Connecticut: The Globe Pequot Press, 2004

Simpson, Dorothy. *The Maine Islands in History and Legend.* Philadelphia, Pennsylvania: J. P. Lippencott, 1960

Singh, Simon. *The Code Book.* New York, New York: Delacorte Press, 2001

Sinkankas, John. *Mineralogy – A first course*. New York, New York: D. Van Nostrand Co., 1966

Skinner, Charles M. *American Myths and Legends*. Philadelphia, Pennsylvania: J. B. Lippencott Co., 1993

Skinner, Charles M. *Myths and Legends of our own Land, Volumes 1 and 2*. Philadelphia, Pennsylvania: J. B. Lippincott Co., 1896

Smith, Alan. *Introduction to Treasure Hunting*. Harrisburg, Pennsylvania: Stackpole Co., 1971

Smith, Marion Jaques. *A History of Maine from Wilderness to Statehood*. Portland, Maine: Falmouth Publishing House, 1949

Snow, Edward Rowe. *Fantastic Folklore and Fact*. New York, New York: Dodd, Mead & Co., 1968

Snow, Edward, Rowe. *Fury of the Seas*. New York, New York: Dodd, Mead & Co., 1964

Snow, Edward, Rowe. *Ghosts, Gales, and Gold*. New York, New York: Dodd, Mead & Co., 1972

Snow, Edward Rowe. *Great Gales and Dire Disasters*. New York, New York: Dodd, Mead & Co., 1952

Snow, Edward Rowe. *Great Storms & Famous Shipwrecks of the New England Coast*. Boston, Massachusetts: Yankee Publishing Co., 1946

Snow, Edward Rowe. *Incredible Mysteries and Legends of the Sea*. New York, New York: Dodd, Mead & Co., 1967

Snow, Edward Rowe. *Legends of the New England Coast*. New York, New York: Dodd, Mead & Co., 1957

Snow, Edward Rowe. *Mysteries and Adventures along the Atlantic Coast*. New York, New York: Dodd, Mead & Co., 1948

Snow, Edward, Rowe. *New England Tales of Land and Sea*. New York, New York: Dodd, Mead & Co., 1968

Snow, Edward Rowe. *Piracy, Mutiny & Murder*. New York, New York: Dodd, Mead & Co., 1959

Snow, Edward Rowe. *Pirates and Buccaneers of the Atlantic Coast*. Boston, Massachusetts: The Yankee Publishing Co., 1944

Snow, Edward Rowe. *Secrets of the North Atlantic*. New York, New York: Dodd, Mead, and Co., 1950

Snow, Edward Rowe. *Supernatural Mysteries & Other Tales*. New York, New York: Dodd, Mead & Co., 1974

Snow, Edward Rowe. *Storms and Shipwrecks of New England*. Boston, Massachusetts: The Yankee Publishing Co., 1943

Snow, Edward Rowe. *Strange Tales from Nova Scotia to Cape Hatteras*. New York, New York: Dodd, Mead & Co., 1949

Snow, Edward Rowe. *The Lighthouses of New England*. New York, New York: Dodd, Mead & Co.,1945

Snow, Edward Rowe. *True Tales of Buried Treasure*. New York, New York: Dodd, Mead & Co., 1952

Sobol, Donald J. *Great Sea Stories*. New York, New York: Scholastic Book Services, 1975

Speare, Eva A. *New Hampshire Folk Tales*. Canaan, New Hampshire: Phoenix Publishing, 1974

Stevens, C.A. *The Knockabout Club in the Woods*. Boston, Massachusetts: Estes & Lauriat, 1882

Stevens, C.J. *Next Bend in the River*. Phillips, Maine: John Wade Publishing, 1989

Stier, Maggie & McArdow, Ron. *Into the Mountains*. Boston, Massachusetts: Appalachian Mountain Club Books, 1995

Stirling, N.B. *Treasure under the sea*. New York, New York: Doubleday & Co., 1957

Sylvester, Herbert Milton. *Ye Romance of Casco Bay*. Boston, Massachusetts: Stanhope Press, 1904

Taft, Lewis A. *Profile of Old New England, Yankee Legends, Tales and Folklore*. New York, New York: Dodd, Mead & Co., 1965

Taylor, Alan. *Liberty Men and Great Proprietors*. Williamsburg, Virginia: University of North Carolina, 1990

Taylor, Wagner. *Pieces of Eight*. New York, New York: E.P. Dutton & Co., Inc., 1966

Thaxter, Celia. *Among the Isles of Shoals.*Sanbornville, New Hampshire: Wake-Brook House, 1873

Thompson, M. B. E. C. J. S. *The Mystery and Lore of Monsters*, New York, New York: The MacMillan Co., 1931

Verde, Thomas A. *Maine Ghosts and Legends: 26 Encounters with the Supernatural*. Camden, Maine: Down East Books, 1989

Verrill, A. Hyatt. *Along New England Shores*. New York, New York: G.P. Putnam's Sons, 1936

Verrill, A. Hyatt. *They Found Gold and the Story of Successful Treasure Hunts*. New York, New York: G. P. Putnam's Sons, 1936

Whipple, A. B. C. *Pirate: Rascals of the Spanish Main.* New York, New York: Doubleday & Co., 1957

Wilkins, Harold T. *Pirate Treasure.* New York, New York: E. P. Dutton & Co., 1937

Workers of the Federal Writer's Project of the Works Progress Administration for the State of Vermont. *Vermont: A guide to the Green Mountain State.* Cambridge, Massachusetts: The Riverside Press, 1937

Young, Hazel. *Islands of New England.* New York, New York: Little, Brown & Co., 1945

Website Resources

http://apod.nasa.gov
www.bostonmagazine.com
www.coinworld.com
www.daac.gsfc.nasa.gov
www.davistownmuseum.org
http:/history.rays-place.com
http://home.gwi.net/amcmaine
www.kingquest.com
www.newadvent.org
www.newsnavy.mil
www.rootsweb.com
www.state.me.us
www.trails.com

Newspaper Resources

Maugh, Thomas H. "Captain Kidd's Wreck may give view of pirate life." Bangor, Maine: Bangor Dairly News, April 29-30, 2000, page D1

Rumsey, Barbara. "Treasure, Part 1 and 2." Boothbay Harbor, Maine: Boothbay Register, April 26, May 3, 2001

Index